RAY COMFORT

Bridge-Logos *Publishers*

Gainesville, Florida 32614 USA

Who is the Lord of the Ring?

Published by:
Bridge-Logos Publishers
P.O. Box 141630
Gainesville, FL 32614, USA
www.bridgelogos.com

Edited by Lynn Copeland

Design and production by Genesis Group, Inc.
(www.genesiswebsite.com)

Illustrations by Richard Gunther

Cover by Joe Potter (joepotter.com)

Printed in the United States of America

ISBN 0-88270-892-9

The text used in this Bible is a "Comfort-able KJV"—a sensitively
revised King James Version, in which archaic words have been
simplified to make the Gospel of John more understandable.

Presented to:

_____

_____

From:

Community Life Church
315 E. 11th St.
Lockport, IL 60441
815-836-3600
www.forministry.com/60441CLC

On:

_____

"For everyone who does evil
hates the light, and does not come to the light,
lest his deeds should be exposed."

JOHN 3:20

Contents

· · · · · · · · · ·

Foreword

. . . .

I USED to think the Bible was written for "holier than thou" religious fanatics. I still do. They need to read it because they don't understand it. If they really understood the Bible, they'd stop thinking they were holier than thou and give up their religion. That's what Jesus told them to do!

I know now that the Bible was also written for non-religious people like you and me. It is the most intriguing, exciting, frightening, and life changing book on the planet. It was written by God and answers your most difficult questions. It knows your secrets and tells your future with perfect accuracy. I'm not trying to scare you—just trying to prepare you. If you will trust it and obey it, God will change you from the inside out.

This book is just part of the Bible, and is specifically about the Lord of Lords. You will find that there is nothing "religious" about Him. I hope God touches you through this wonderful book known as the Gospel of John.

KIRK CAMERON

Preface

. . . .

T HE BIBLE tells us that a man named Philip saw someone reading the Scriptures. We pick up the story in Acts 8:30,31:

> And Philip ran there to him, and heard him read the prophet Isaiah, and said, Do you understand what you read? And he said, How can I, except some man should guide me? And he invited Philip to come up and sit with him.

It is my hope that you will let me "sit" with you, and perhaps guide you with a few thoughts relevant to the most important subject in your life—your eternal salvation.

The Gospel
of JESUS CHRIST,
the King *of* kings
& Lord *of* lords,
according to
the apostle
John

Come, See the Lamb

I N the beginning was the Word, and the Word was with God, and the Word was God.

2 The same was in the beginning with God.

3 All things were made by him; and without him was not anything made that was made.

4 In him was life; and the life was the light of men.

• •

1:1 The "Word" was "in the beginning" with God. Let's therefore go to the "beginning" (Genesis chapter 1) to see the Word: "In the beginning God created the heaven and the earth. And the earth was without form, and void; and darkness was upon the face of the deep. And the Spirit of God moved upon the face of the waters. And God said, Let there be light: and there was light." Can you see the Word? It was manifest when God *spoke*. It was God's voice that brought light into being, and the Bible tells us that this same Word (His voice) became flesh in the person Jesus of Nazareth (see verse 14). Jesus not only was *with* God, He *is* God.

The prophet Isaiah, 700 years before Christ, spoke of the birth of the Savior and called Him "the mighty God": "For unto us a child is born, unto us a son is given: and the government shall be upon his shoulder: and his name shall be called Wonderful, Counselor, the mighty God, the everlasting Father, the Prince of Peace" (Isaiah 9:6).

1:3 Nothing "evolved" of itself. The Bible makes it very clear that *all* things were made by Jesus Christ, "who is the image of the invisible God," before He was manifest in human form: "For by him were all things created, that are in heaven, and that are in earth, visible and invisible, whether they be thrones, or dominions, or principalities, or powers: all things were created by him, and for him. He is before all things, and by him all things consist" (Colossians 1:15–17).

1:4 The "Word" had life in Himself. This is because He is the very *source* of life. John described Jesus as "the Word of life...which was from the beginning": "We have seen it and testify to it, and we proclaim to you the eternal

5 And the light shines in darkness; and the darkness did not comprehend it.

6 There was a man sent from God, whose name was John.

7 The same came for a witness, to bear witness of the Light, that all men through him might believe.

8 He was not that Light, but was sent to bear witness of that Light.

9 That was the true Light, which lights every man who comes into the world.

10 He was in the world, and the world was made by him, and the world did not know him.

11 He came to his own, and his own did not receive him.

. . . .

life, which was with the Father and has appeared to us" (1 John 1:1,2). Look at the unprecedented and unique claims of Jesus about being life itself: "I am the way, the truth, and the *life*," "I have come that they might have *life*," "I am the resurrection and the *life*." The apostle Paul (who wrote most of the New Testament) spoke of "Christ, who is our *life*," while John wrote, "He who has the Son has *life*." All who accept Jesus receive the *life* of God, and will "have the light of *life*" (John 8:12). It is the life of God in the believer that overcomes the power of death.

1:6   John the Baptist is an important figure in each of the four New Testament Gospels (the books of Matthew, Mark, Luke, and John). He is known as the forerunner to Jesus the Messiah.

1:10   This Light who came into the world, Jesus of Nazareth, was the Creator of whales and birds, dogs and cows, flowers and thunder, the sun and moon, and the infinite galaxies. He made the Grand Canyon, snowflakes, apples, and the human eye, with its 137,000,000 light-sensitive cells. He gave your eye the ability to automatically blink and keep it cleansed of impurities. He was the Maker of the incredible brain with which you are processing these words. He made the hands that are holding this book. He created the heart that is pumping your life's blood through your flesh. *All* things were made by Him. He was the Creator; He became a person, "and the world did not know Him." Do you *know* Him? If you don't, then you confirm the truth of this verse. You are His creation and yet you don't know Him.

If you find it hard to comprehend the deity of Jesus Christ (that He is God), you are not alone. A skeptic named General Lew Wallace once determined to disprove the "myth" of the Christian faith. After two years of studying the New Testament, he dropped to his knees and cried out to Jesus of Nazareth, "My Lord and my God!" He then went on to write the legendary novel *Ben Hur*—the story of the life of Christ.

1:11   His own people, the Jews, didn't receive Him. The first time He publicly read from the Scriptures they tried to kill Him (see Luke 4:29).

12 But as many as received him, to them he gave power to become the sons of God, even to those who believe on his name:

13 Who were born, not of blood, nor of the will of the flesh, nor of the will of man, but of God.

14 And the Word was made flesh, and dwelt among us (and we beheld his glory, the glory as of the only begotten of the Father), full of grace and truth.

15 John bore witness of him, and cried, saying, This was he of whom I spoke, He who comes after me is preferred before me: for he was before me.

16 And of his fullness we have all received, and grace for grace.

17 For the law was given by Moses, but grace and truth came by Jesus Christ.

18 No man has seen God at any time; the only begotten Son, who is in the bosom of the Father, he has declared him.

· ·

1:12   Eternal salvation comes through trusting Jesus Christ.

1:13   When someone becomes a Christian, he is born of God. He is not converted by arguments or (as some claim) "by the Bible." Early Christians didn't have the New Testament as we know it. There was no such thing as the printing press, and many couldn't read. Instead, they were converted by the power of the message of the gospel, and came to know God through the Holy Spirit.

1:14   "Only begotten" means one of a kind—utterly unique.

1:17   God gave us the Law of Moses to bring us to the grace of God that is in Jesus Christ (see Galatians 3:24). The Law (the Ten Commandments) shows us God's perfect standard, so that we will see our need of His forgiveness. For the Ten Commandments, see page 112.

1:18   God has manifested Himself in different forms to different people. He spoke to Moses through the burning bush, and He has revealed Himself to others in visions, in angelic forms, and in dreams. But no man has ever seen the very essence of God at any time. When Moses asked to see God's glory, God hid him in the cleft of a rock, and Moses was allowed to look at where God had been. The experience of looking at where God had passed by caused the face of Moses to so shine that the children of Israel couldn't even look at him. Moses had to cover his face (see Exodus 34:33).

It is interesting to note that God told Moses that His "goodness" would pass by, and that is what he could look upon. Strange though it may sound, it is the goodness of God that would instantly kill sinful man. To understand this, think

19 And this is the record of John, when the Jews sent priests and Levites from Jerusalem to ask him, Who are you?

20 And he confessed, and denied not; but confessed, I am not the Christ.

21 And they asked him, What then? are you Elijah? And he said, I am not. Are you that prophet? And he answered, No.

22 Then they said to him, Who are you? that we may give an answer to those who sent us. What do you say of yourself?

23 He said, I am the voice of one crying in the wilderness, Make straight the way of the Lord, as the prophet Isaiah said.

24 And those who were sent were of the Pharisees.

25 And they asked him, and said to him, Why do you baptize then, if you are not that Christ, nor Elijah, neither that prophet?

26 John answered them, saying, I baptize with water: but there stands one among you, whom you do not know;

27 It is he who, coming after me, is preferred before me, whose shoe's strap I am not worthy to unloose.

28 These things were done in Bethabara beyond Jordan, where John was baptizing.

29 The next day John saw Jesus coming to him, and said, Behold the Lamb of God, who takes away the sin of the world.

30 This is he of whom I said, After me comes a man who is preferred before me: for he was before me.

• •

in terms of civil law. An essentially good judge cannot entertain any form of evil. He *must* pronounce swift judgment upon a vicious criminal. If the goodness of God was manifested to sinful man, it would devour him in the same way fire devours a dead and dry leaf. It is its very nature to do so.

1:23   The ministry of John the Baptist was foretold by the prophet Isaiah (Isaiah 40:3).

1:24   The Pharisees were a group of specially observant and influential Jews, mainly in Palestine, from the second century B.C. to the first century A.D.

1:29   When the Israelites were slaves in Egypt, God told them to take the blood of a spotless lamb and put it on the doorposts of their homes. As He was bringing judgment upon the Egyptians, when He saw the blood, His judgment would pass over those in the house. (The Jewish Passover commemorates this event.) This is a picture of what God would eventually do through the coming Messiah. Jesus of Nazareth was the perfect Lamb provided by God who was slain to take away the sin of the world. The judgment of God passes over all who trust in Jesus' shed blood.

31 And I did not know him: but that he should be made manifest to Israel, therefore I have come baptizing with water.

32 And John bore record, saying, I saw the Spirit descending from heaven like a dove, and it remained upon him.

33 And I did not know him: but he who sent me to baptize with water, the same said to me, Upon whom you shall see the Spirit descending, and remaining on him, the same is he who baptizes with the Holy Spirit.

34 And I saw, and bore record that this is the Son of God.

35 Again the next day after John stood, and two of his disciples;

36 And looking upon Jesus as he walked, he said, Behold the Lamb of God!

37 And the two disciples heard him speak, and they followed Jesus.

38 Then Jesus turned and saw them following, and said to them, What do you seek? They said to him, Rabbi (which is to say, being interpreted, Master), where do you dwell?

39 He said to them, Come and see. They came and saw where he dwelt, and remained with him that day: for it was about the tenth hour.

40 One of the two who heard John speak, and followed him, was Andrew, Simon Peter's brother.

41 He first found his own brother Simon, and said to him, We have found the Messiah, which is, being interpreted, the Christ.

42 And he brought him to Jesus. And when Jesus beheld him, he said, You are Simon the son of Jonah: you shall be called Cephas, which is by interpretation, A stone.

43 The following day Jesus went forth into Galilee, and found Philip, and said to him, Follow me.

44 Now Philip was of Bethsaida, the city of Andrew and Peter.

45 Philip found Nathanael, and said to him, We have found him of whom Moses in the law, and the prophets, wrote, Jesus of Nazareth, the son of Joseph.

46 And Nathanael said to him, Can any good thing come out of Nazareth? Philip said to him, Come and see.

· ·

1:39 The Jewish day began at 6 A.M., so this was about 4:00 P.M.

1:41 When you find everlasting life in Christ, the first thing you want to do is tell your loved ones. See also verse 45.

47 Jesus saw Nathanael coming to him, and said of him, Behold an Israelite indeed, in whom is no guile!

48 Nathanael said to him, Where do you know me from? Jesus answered and said to him, Before Philip called you, when you were under the fig tree, I saw you.

49 Nathanael answered and said to him, Rabbi, you are the Son of God; you are the King of Israel.

50 Jesus answered and said to him, Because I said to you, I saw you under the fig tree, do you believe? you shall see greater things than these.

51 And he said to him, Verily, verily, I say to you, Hereafter you shall see heaven open, and the angels of God ascending and descending upon the Son of man.

. . . .

1:46   Nathanael's question is a typical reaction of the contemporary world to those who follow the Savior. To the cynical, Christians are intellectual wimps, prudes, rejects—unlearned cripples who need some sort of crutch to get them through life. So it is understandable for them to ask, "Can any good thing come out of Christianity?" Philip merely answered Nathanael's cynicism with the same thing Jesus said to Andrew—"Come and see." This is the challenge to any skeptic: *Come and see*. Atheist, come and see. Intellectual, come and see. Just come with a humble and teachable heart, and you who are sightless *will* see and know that this Man from Nazareth is the Son of God.

1:48   Perhaps you have sat "under a fig tree" and uttered a secret prayer. You may have whispered, "God, where are You?" Perhaps the fact that you are reading this is God's answer to that prayer. Look at this promise: "Draw near to God, and he will draw near to you. Cleanse your hands, you sinners; and purify your hearts, you double minded" (James 4:8).

1:51   "Verily," which means "truly," is used twice for emphasis. Jesus is perhaps referring to Genesis 28:12, in which Jacob dreamed of angels ascending and descending on a ladder from heaven. The phrase the "Son of Man" occurs 86 times in the New Testament and once in the Old Testament (Daniel 7:13), and refers to Jesus.

CHAPTER 2

Whip of Cords

A ND the third day there was a marriage in Cana of Galilee; and the mother of Jesus was there:

2 And both Jesus was called, and his disciples, to the marriage.

3 And when they wanted wine, the mother of Jesus said to him, They have no wine.

4 Jesus said to her, Woman, what have I to do with you? my hour has not yet come.

5 His mother said to the servants, Whatever he says to you, do it.

6 And there were set there six waterpots of stone, after the manner of the purifying of the Jews, containing two or three firkins apiece.

7 Jesus said to them, Fill the waterpots with water. And they filled them up to the brim.

8 And he said to them, Draw out now, and take to the master of the feast. And they took it.

9 When the ruler of the feast had tasted the water that was made wine, and did not know from where it

. . . .

2:4 This was an expression Jesus used a number of times, speaking of His coming death on the cross.

2:5 Those who esteem Mary should heed her words. She said to do what Jesus said, and Jesus said that we *must* be born again to enter the kingdom of God. See John 3:3.

2:6 This amount is equivalent to twenty or thirty gallons.

came (but the servants who drew the water knew); the master of the feast called the bridegroom,

10 And said to him, Every man at the beginning sets forth good wine; and when men have well drunk, then that which is worse: but you have kept the good wine until now.

11 This beginning of miracles Jesus did in Cana of Galilee, and manifested forth his glory; and his disciples believed on him.

12 After this he went down to Capernaum, he, and his mother, and his brethren, and his disciples: and they continued there not many days.

13 And the Jews' Passover was at hand, and Jesus went up to Jerusalem,

14 And found in the temple those who sold oxen and sheep and doves, and the changers of money sitting:

15 And when he had made a whip of small cords, he drove them all out of the temple, and the sheep, and the oxen; and poured out the changers' money, and overthrew the tables;

16 And said to those who sold doves, Take these things away; do not make my Father's house a house of merchandise.

17 And his disciples remembered that it was written, The zeal of your house has eaten me up.

18 Then the Jews answered and said to him, What sign do you show to us, seeing that you do these things?

19 Jesus answered and said to them, Destroy this temple, and in three days I will raise it up.

. . . .

2:11   Some claim that did Jesus miracles when He was a child. He was said to have become angry with some other children and turned them into goats. He also supposedly turned clay into pigeons. This verse proves such talk to be bogus.

2:14   According to the historian Josephus, over 250,000 animals were sacrificed each Passover. It was the priests who sold licenses to the venders, so the market must have been lucrative.

2:16   Jesus referred to God as His Father 53 times. Such talk was radical. Up until this time God was referred to as the "Father" only of the nation of Israel.

2:17   Jesus was without sin. His anger was righteous indignation toward Israel's equivalent of money-hungry televangelists. Who in his right mind cannot commend such a noble action?

20 Then the Jews said, This temple took forty-six years to build, and you will raise it up in three days?

21 But he spoke of the temple of his body.

22 Therefore when he was risen from the dead, his disciples remembered that he had said this to them; and they believed the scripture, and the word which Jesus had said.

23 Now when he was in Jerusalem at the Passover, in the feast day, many believed in his name, when they saw the miracles which he did.

24 But Jesus did not commit himself to them, because he knew all men,

25 And needed not that any should testify of man: for he knew what was in man.

CHAPTER 3

Light Haters

THERE was a man of the Pharisees, named Nicodemus, a ruler of the Jews:

2 The same came to Jesus by night, and said to him, Rabbi, we know that you are a teacher come from God: for no man can do these miracles that you do, except God be with him.

3 Jesus answered and said to him, Verily, verily, I say to you, Except a man be born again, he cannot see the kingdom of God.

4 Nicodemus said to him, How can a man be born when he is old? can he enter the second time into his mother's womb, and be born?

· ·

3:3 The phrase "born-again Christian" is redundant and is detrimental to the cause of the gospel. It is like saying, "He's a medical doctor physician." If someone is a physician, he is a medical doctor. If a person is a Christian, he has been born again, and if he has been born again, he is a Christian. To say "born-again Christian" implies that there is a category of Christians who haven't been born again, which is not true.

3:4 Like Nicodemus, many people have no concept of what it means to be born again. He understandably thought that Jesus was referring to natural human birth, in which we are surrounded by water (see verse 5). Others see the experience as being a spiritual "tingle" when they think of God, or a warm fuzzy feeling when they enter a church building. Or maybe they believe that one is born again when one is "christened" or "confirmed." It's important to understand it accurately because Jesus said three times in these verses (3–7) that the new birth is absolutely essential for sinners to enter heaven. If they are not born again, they will not enter the kingdom of God.

Peter, when writing to Christians about their salvation, said they were "born again, not of corruptible seed, but of incorruptible, by the word of God, which lives and abides forever" (1 Peter 1:23). How is one born again? Simply through repentance toward God and faith in the Lord Jesus Christ. Admit your sins and

5 Jesus answered, Verily, verily, I say to you, Except a man be born of water and of the Spirit, he cannot enter into the kingdom of God.

6 That which is born of the flesh is flesh; and that which is born of the Spirit is spirit.

7 Do not marvel that I said to you, You must be born again.

8 The wind blows where it wishes, and you hear the sound of it, but cannot tell where it comes from and where it goes: so is everyone who is born of the Spirit.

9 Nicodemus answered and said to him, How can these things be?

10 Jesus answered and said to him, Are you a master of Israel, and do not know these things?

11 Verily, verily, I say to you, We speak what we do know, and testify what we have seen; and you do not receive our witness.

12 If I have told you earthly things, and you do not believe, how shall you believe if I tell you of heavenly things?

13 And no man has ascended up to heaven, but he who came down from heaven, even the Son of man who is in heaven.

14 And as Moses lifted up the serpent in the wilderness, even so must the Son of man be lifted up:

• •

turn from them, and trust in Jesus alone for your eternal salvation. When you do, you will be "born of the Spirit" (verse 8)—you receive spiritual life through the Holy Spirit who comes to live within you.

When you are born again, you become a "new creature in Christ" (2 Corinthians 5:17). You will come out of darkness into light, out of death into life. The Word of God will come alive to you. God will give you a spiritual heart transplant, so you will have a love for other Christians and for God, and will long to do those things that please Him. The new birth is so radical, you will shake your head in wonder for the rest of eternity.

3:13 It would make sense for a great man to say, "For this purpose I was born." However, Jesus speaks here of His *preexistence* in heaven. He said that He "*came down*" from heaven. He was either insane, a liar, or was speaking the truth.

3:14 While the Israelites were wandering in the desert, they complained bitterly against God so He sent "fiery serpents" among them. Many Israelites were bitten by the poisonous serpents and died. As they admitted that they had sinned, God gave them a means of salvation: they were to look up to a bronze serpent that Moses had placed on a pole. Those who had been bitten and were doomed to die could look at the bronze serpent and live (Numbers

15 That whoever believes in him should not perish, but have eternal life.

16 For God so loved the world, that he gave his only begotten Son, that whoever believes in him should not perish, but have everlasting life.

17 For God did not send his Son into the world to condemn the world; but that the world through him might be saved.

18 He who believes on him is not condemned: but he who does not believe is condemned already, because he has not believed in the name of the only begotten Son of God.

• •

21:6–9). In these verses, Jesus specifically cited this Old Testament passage in reference to salvation from sin. When Jesus is lifted up on a cross, those sinners who look to Him will live and will be saved from the curse of death.

3:16   This is perhaps the most well-known Bible verse. It tells us that God was motivated by love when He became flesh and suffered and died on the cross. Jesus paid the penalty for our sin, so that we could be granted everlasting life. All who believe in, trust in, and rely upon Jesus Christ will not perish under the wrath of God's Law. They will have "fullness of joy" and "pleasures forevermore." There is a wise saying: "If it seems too good to be true, it probably is." This is valid when dealing with mankind, but it is not the case with the promises of God.

Imagine if I said that I was a billionaire and would give you $1 million when you finished reading this book. As a token of good faith, I will give you $100,000 now as a down payment. As I put the $100,000 in your hand, you would say, "Wow! This guy means what he says." The down payment proves the sincerity of the promise of $1 million. God promises everlasting life to all who trust in the Savior. As a token of good faith, He gives us His Holy Spirit. This is the meaning of Ephesians 1:13,14: "you were sealed with that Holy Spirit of promise, who is the earnest of our inheritance . . ."

3:18   Anyone who is not trusting in the Savior is *already* condemned. Sinners are not condemned because they don't believe in Jesus. They are condemned because they have sinned—committed adultery, murdered, stolen, lied, etc. This concept can be understood by considering why a man perishes if he jumps out of a plane without a parachute. Had he trusted in a parachute, he would have been saved. So in one sense it is true that he perished  because he didn't put on a parachute. However, the *primary* reason he died was because he broke the law of gravity. In the same way, sinners are condemned because they have broken the Law of God. Had a sinner "put on the

19 And this is the condemnation, that light has come into the world, and men loved darkness rather than light, because their deeds were evil.

20 For everyone who does evil hates the light, and does not come to the light, lest his deeds should be exposed.

21 But he who does truth comes to the light, that his deeds may

. . . .

Lord Jesus Christ" (Romans 13:14), he would have been saved; but because he refused to repent, he will suffer the full consequences of his sin. Sin is not "failing to believe in Jesus"; sin is "transgression of the Law" (1 John 3:4).

3:19   The truth of this can be seen in what the world enjoys as entertainment. Advertise any movie as having an "adult" theme—with lots of lust, avid adultery, rampant rape, grasping greed, and vicious violence—and as sure as hell, it will sell well. If you think otherwise, take the time to stroll through a video store and look at the cover titles and graphics. Our own heart's desires condemn us. We have as much desire for the "light" of righteousness as a four-year-old boy has for the word "bath." It is the darkness of sin that we naturally crave.

3:20   If you are not a Christian, try to put your finger on the real reason why not. Isn't it that you prefer your way to God's way? One way to clarify this is to ask yourself, "What would I have to give up if I became a Christian?" Make a list and ask yourself, "Is this worth hell for eternity?"

Here is a thought-provoking question: Would you sell one of your eyes for a million dollars? Would you sell both for fifty million? No one in his right mind would. You eyes are priceless, yet they are merely the windows of your soul. Your soul's value is inestimable. Yet are you willing to be damned for eternity in exchange for a few fleeting moments of sinful pleasure? Look at what Jesus said about God's place of punishment: "If your eye offends you, pluck it out: it is better for you to enter into the kingdom of God with one eye, than having two eyes to be cast into hell fire: where their worm does not die, and the fire is not quenched" (Mark 9:47,48). How's your tolerance for pain—high or low? Do you enjoy the dentist's drill when it hits a nerve? Do you like spinal pain? Do you enjoy the feeling of a broken bone? Is it pleasant for you to have your finger slammed in a door or to burn it on a hot appliance? No one in his right mind likes pain, and yet you are running toward the pain of hell as though it were the joy of heaven. Please, take God's warning seriously. The agonies of this life are but trivial inconveniences compared to what is in store for those who have transgressed God's Law. Death will bring the full penalty for sin.

Listen to your fears. Flee from the wrath to come, to the safety of the Savior. Don't put off your eternal salvation for another minute. Confess and turn from your sins, then put your trust in Jesus Christ. For further information on how to do this, see John 6:47 comment.

be made manifest, that they are done in God.

22 After these things Jesus and his disciples came into the land of Judea; and there he tarried with them, and baptized.

23 And John also was baptizing in Aenon near to Salim, because there was much water there: and they came, and were baptized.

24 For John was not yet cast into prison.

25 Then there arose a question between some of John's disciples and the Jews about purifying.

26 And they came to John, and said to him, Rabbi, he who was with you beyond Jordan, to whom you bear witness, behold, the same baptizes, and all men come to him.

27 John answered and said, A man can receive nothing, except it be given him from heaven.

28 You yourselves bear me witness, that I said, I am not the Christ, but that I am sent before him.

29 He who has the bride is the bridegroom: but the friend of the bridegroom, who stands and hears him, rejoices greatly because of the bridegroom's voice: therefore my joy is fulfilled.

30 He must increase, but I must decrease.

31 He who comes from above is above all: he who is of the earth is earthly, and speaks of the earth: he who comes from heaven is above all.

32 And what he has seen and heard, that he testifies; and no man receives his testimony.

33 He who has received his testimony has set to his seal that God is true.

. . . .

3:36 God's wrath abides on you. Your sin is a lightning rod for divine indignation. Did you know this? Perhaps you think God is a benevolent father-figure (as many people do). However, the Bible teaches that, until we come to the Savior, each of us is an enemy of God through our wicked works (Colossians 1:21). We are called "children of wrath" (Ephesians 2:3), and every time we sin we store up God's wrath, which will be revealed on the Day of Judgment (Romans 2:5).

If you've ever seen a freeway chase on the news, you've probably thought, "What's wrong with this man? Every time he violates traffic laws he gets himself more jail time. He can't escape the law. There's a helicopter tracking his every move. Why doesn't he just give up?"

You could be asked the same question. Every time you sin, you are bringing more wrath upon yourself. You can't get away from God's Law. His eye is in every place. Why don't you just give up?

34 For he whom God has sent speaks the words of God: for God does not give the Spirit by measure to him.

35 The Father loves the Son, and has given all things into his hand.

36 He who believes on the Son has everlasting life: and he who does not believe the Son shall not see life; but the wrath of God abides on him.

CHAPTER 4

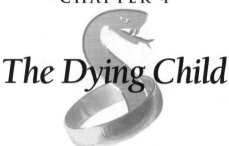

The Dying Child

T HEREFORE when the Lord knew how the Pharisees had heard that Jesus made and baptized more disciples than John,

2 (Though Jesus himself did not baptize, but his disciples,)

3 He left Judea, and departed again into Galilee.

4 And he needed to go through Samaria.

5 Then he came to a city of Samaria, which is called Sychar, near to the parcel of ground that Jacob gave to his son Joseph.

6 Now Jacob's well was there. Jesus therefore, being wearied with his journey, sat thus on the well: and it was about the sixth hour.

7 A woman of Samaria came to draw water: Jesus said to her, Give me to drink.

8 (For his disciples had gone away to the city to buy food.)

9 Then the woman of Samaria said to him, How is it that you, being a Jew, ask drink of me, a woman of Samaria? for the Jews have no dealings with the Samaritans.

10 Jesus answered and said to her, If you knew the gift of God, and who it is who said to you, Give me to drink; you would have asked of him, and he would have given you living water.

• •

4:4 The insinuation is that Jesus deliberately went through Samaria to speak with one woman about her eternal salvation. Considering how many people live on the face of the earth, it is amazing that God would have any concern for the individual. However, He does. He even knows how many hairs are on our heads (Matthew 10:30).

4:6 This was at about noon.

4:9 Samaritans were people whom the king of Assyria had brought from various places to settle in the cities of Samaria. These strangers intermarried with the Jews remaining in the land, blending their old idolatry with parts of the Jewish religion.

11 The woman said to him, Sir, you have nothing to draw with, and the well is deep: from where then do you get that living water?

12 Are you greater than our father Jacob, who gave us the well, and drank from it himself, and his children, and his cattle?

13 Jesus answered and said to her, Whoever drinks of this water shall thirst again:

14 But whoever drinks of the water that I shall give him shall never thirst; but the water that I shall give him shall be in him a well of water springing up into everlasting life.

15 The woman said to him, Sir, give me this water, that I may not thirst, nor come here to draw.

16 Jesus said to her, Go, call your husband, and come here.

17 The woman answered and said, I have no husband. Jesus said to her, You have well said, I have no husband:

18 For you have had five husbands; and he whom you now have is not your husband: in that you said truly.

19 The woman said to him, Sir, I perceive that you are a prophet.

20 Our fathers worshiped in this mountain; and you say that in Jerusalem is the place where men ought to worship.

21 Jesus said to her, Woman, believe me, the hour comes when you shall neither in this mountain, nor yet at Jerusalem, worship

· ·

4:10 Relatively few in the world know that the "gift of God is eternal life through Jesus Christ our Lord" (Romans 6:23). The great error of "religion" is the teaching that mankind can earn eternal life through good works. No one can *earn* a gift.

If this woman knew who Jesus was, she would have asked for immortality. If this perishing world knew who Jesus was, they would fall at His feet to be saved from death and receive eternal life.

4:14 The Bible says that we drink iniquity (sin) like water. Until we come to Jesus Christ that thirst is unquenchable.

4:14 Jesus' words are strange coming from Someone whom many people claim was merely a moral teacher. He is saying that He has water to give that provides everlasting life.

4:18 God knows our secret sins. Nothing is hidden from His eyes: "O LORD, you have searched me, and known me. You know my sitting down and my rising up, you understand my thought afar off. You comprehend my path and my lying down, and are acquainted with all my ways. For there is not a word in my tongue, but, lo, O LORD, you know it altogether" (Psalm 139:1–4).

the Father.

22 You worship what you do not know: we worship what we do know: for salvation is of the Jews.

23 But the hour comes, and now is, when the true worshipers shall worship the Father in spirit and in truth: for the Father seeks such to worship him.

24 God is a Spirit: and those who worship him must worship him in spirit and in truth.

25 The woman said to him, I know that Messiah comes, who is called Christ: when he comes, he will tell us all things.

26 Jesus said to her, I who speak to you am he.

• •

4:24   God is a Spirit. He is unseen. Those who find it difficult to believe in something they can't see should realize that life itself is invisible. It is life in the body that makes it move. If the unseen force of life leaves because of death, the body becomes just an empty shell. God is the invisible source of all life.

Although God does not have a physical body, the Bible uses anthropomorphism to help us understand His nature. Anthropomorphism is the attribution of human qualities to God, such as: "The *hand* of the Lord was upon me," or "The *eye* of the Lord is in every place beholding the evil and the good."

Likewise, when the Bible speaks of Adam as being made in God's "image" (His likeness), it means human beings have some of His attributes. We are different from animals. Even as fallen human beings, we are aware of our "being." God is called "I AM," and we understand that "we are." Among other unique characteristics, we have an innate ability to appreciate God's creation. What animal gazes with awe at a sunset, or at the magnificence of the Grand Canyon? What animal obtains joy from the sounds of music or takes the time to form itself into an orchestra? We are also moral beings. What animal sets up court systems and apportions justice to its fellow creatures? While birds and other creatures have instincts to create (nests, etc.), we have the ability to uncover the hidden laws of electricity. We can utilize the law of aerodynamics to transport ourselves around the globe. We also have the God-given ability to appreciate the *value* of creation. We unearth the hidden treasures  of gold, silver, diamonds, and oil and make use of them for our own benefit. Only humans have the unique ability to appreciate God for His incredible creation, and a spirit with which to respond to Him.

4:25   *Messiah* means "anointed one" (the Greek equivalent is "Christ"). Jesus of Nazareth claimed to be the Messiah, the great Deliverer who was promised in the Scriptures (see Luke 18:31–33; 22:37; Acts 2:22–39; 26:22,23).

27 And upon this came his disciples, and marveled that he talked with the woman: yet no man said, What do you seek? or, Why do you talk with her?

28 The woman then left her waterpot, and went her way into the city, and said to the men,

29 Come, see a man who told me all things that ever I did: is this not the Christ?

30 Then they went out of the city, and came to him.

31 In the meanwhile his disciples prayed him, saying, Master, eat.

32 But he said to them, I have food to eat that you do not know of.

33 Therefore the disciples said to one another, Has any man brought him anything to eat?

34 Jesus said to them, My food is to do the will of him who sent me, and to finish his work.

35 Do you not say, There are yet four months, and then comes the harvest? behold, I say to you, Lift up your eyes, and look on the fields; for they are already white to harvest.

36 And he who reaps receives wages, and gathers fruit to life eternal: that both he who sows and he who reaps may rejoice together.

37 And in this is that saying true, One sows, and another reaps.

38 I sent you to reap that for which you have not labored: other men labored, and you entered into their labors.

39 And many of the Samaritans of that city believed on him for the saying of the woman, who testified, He told me all that I ever did.

40 So when the Samaritans had come to him, they urged him to stay with them: and he remained there two days.

41 And many more believed because of his own word;

42 And said to the woman, Now we believe, not because of your saying: for we have heard him ourselves, and know that this is

• •

4:28 She left her waterpot. Whatever you are doing in life, set it aside until you are right with God. There is nothing more important than your eternal salvation.

4:32 He was speaking of the joy of doing the will of the Father, who had sent Him to die on the cross as a payment for the sins of the world.

4:39 This woman realized that God sees everything we do, and He even knows our thought-life.

indeed the Christ, the Savior of the world.

43 Now after two days he departed from there, and went into Galilee.

44 For Jesus himself testified that a prophet has no honor in his own country.

45 Then when he had come into Galilee, the Galileans received him, having seen all the things that he did at Jerusalem at the feast: for they also went to the feast.

46 So Jesus came again into Cana of Galilee, where he made the water wine. And there was a certain nobleman, whose son was sick at Capernaum.

47 When he heard that Jesus had come out of Judea into Galilee, he went to him, and urged him to come down and heal his son: for he was at the point of death.

48 Then Jesus said to him, Except you see signs and wonders, you will not believe.

49 The nobleman said to him, Sir, come down before my child dies.

50 Jesus said to him, Go your way; your son lives. And the man believed the word that Jesus had spoken to him, and he went his way.

51 And as he was now going down, his servants met him, and told him, saying, Your son lives.

52 Then he inquired of them the hour when he began to get better. And they said to him, Yesterday at the seventh hour the fever left him.

53 So the father knew that it was at the same hour in which Jesus said to him, Your son lives: and he himself believed, and his whole house.

54 This is again the second miracle that Jesus did, when he had come out of Judea into Galilee.

• •

4:49 Too many people harden their hearts against God when death takes a loved one. The avenue of hardness of heart has a dead end. Let the pains of this life bring you (like this man) to the Savior.

CHAPTER 5

Kill Him

A FTER this there was a feast of the Jews; and Jesus went up to Jerusalem.

2 Now there is at Jerusalem by the sheep market a pool, which is called in the Hebrew tongue Bethesda, having five porches.

3 In these lay a great multitude of sick folk, of blind, lame, paralyzed, waiting for the moving of the water.

4 For an angel went down at a certain season into the pool, and stirred up the water: then whoever stepped in first, after the stirring of the water, was made whole of whatever disease he had.

5 And a certain man was there, who had an infirmity thirty-eight years.

6 When Jesus saw him lie, and knew that he had been now a long time in that condition, he said to him, Will you be made whole?

7 The sick man answered him, Sir, I have no man to put me into the pool when the water is stirred up: but while I am coming, another steps down before me.

8 Jesus said to him, Rise, take up your bed, and walk.

9 And immediately the man was made whole, and took up his bed and walked: and on the same day was the Sabbath.

10 The Jews therefore said to him who was cured, It is the Sabbath day: it is not lawful for you to carry your bed.

• •

5:8 All sinners lay as feeble, fragile, and frail folk, helpless and hopeless, pathetically paralyzed by the devil—"taken captive to do his will" until they respond in faith to Jesus. They are on a deathbed of sin with no one able to help them, until they hear the voice of the Word of God saying: "Arise from the dead, and Christ shall give you light" (Ephesians 5:14). As with this feeble man, those who turn from their sin He will make whole (see verse 14).

11 He answered them, He who made me whole, the same said to me, Take up your bed, and walk.

12 Then they asked him, What man is that who said to you, Take up your bed, and walk?

13 And he who was healed did not know who it was: for Jesus had conveyed himself away, a multitude being in that place.

14 Afterward Jesus found him in the temple, and said to him,

. . . .

5:10   Jesus continually clashed with religious folk, who tried to kill Him because He refused to be held by the shackles of religion. The religious leaders were strict in their outward observance of God's Law. However, inwardly they were hypocrites—and Jesus fearlessly told them so (see Matthew 23:13–33). The Bible prophesied that the Messiah would "magnify the Law and make it honorable" (Isaiah 42:21). The religious leaders in Israel had twisted the Law and caused it to lose its original intent. Jesus brought them (and the common people) back to the reality that God requires "truth in the inward parts." Look at how He brings out the spiritual nature of God's Law in the Sermon on the Mount (Matthew 5):

> "For I say to you, That except your righteousness shall exceed the righteousness of the scribes and Pharisees, you shall in no case enter into the kingdom of heaven. You have heard that it was said by those of old, You shall not kill; and whoever kills shall be in danger of the judgment: But I say to you, That whoever is angry with his brother without a cause shall be in danger of the judgment . . .
>
> You have heard that it was said by those of old, You shall not commit adultery: But I say to you, That whoever looks on a woman to lust after her has already committed adultery with her in his heart . . .
>
> Again you have heard that it was said by those of old, You shall not swear falsely, but shall perform your oaths to the Lord. But I say to you, do not swear at all: neither by heaven, for it is God's throne; nor by the earth, for it is His footstool; nor by Jerusalem, for it is the city of the great King . . .
>
> You have heard that it was said, You shall love your neighbor and hate your enemy. But I say to you, Love your enemies, bless those who curse you, do good to those who hate you, and pray for those who spitefully use you and persecute you; that you may be the children of your Father in heaven: for he makes his sun to rise on the evil and on the good, and sends rain on the just and on the unjust. For if you love those who love you, what reward do you have? do not even the tax collectors do the same? And if you greet your brethren only, what do you do more than others? do not even the tax collectors do so? Be therefore perfect, even as your Father in heaven is perfect."

Behold, you are made whole: sin no more, lest a worse thing come to you.

15 The man departed, and told the Jews that it was Jesus who had made him whole.

16 And therefore did the Jews persecute Jesus, and sought to slay him, because he had done these things on the Sabbath day.

17 But Jesus answered them, My Father works until now, and I work.

18 Therefore the Jews sought the more to kill him, because he not only had broken the Sabbath, but also said that God was his Father, making himself equal with God.

19 Then Jesus answered and said to them, Verily, verily, I say to you, The Son can do nothing of himself, but what he sees the Father do: for whatever things he does, these the Son also does likewise.

• •

5:16 The great enemy of Christianity is religion. That may seem like a contradiction until you understand that religion has been well-defined as "man striving to find peace with God by his own efforts." In Christianity, God reached down to man and made peace Himself, through the cross of Jesus Christ. Most of the Christian martyrs throughout history died at the hands of religious people who killed them in the name of God.

5:18 Jesus claimed to be equal with God because He is God. His human form is often referred to as His *humiliation*. The Bible tells us that Jesus, "being in the form of God, did not think it robbery to be equal with God: but made himself of no reputation, and took upon him the form of a servant, and was made in the likeness of men. And being found in appearance as a man, he humbled himself, and became obedient unto death, even the death of the cross" (Philippians 2:5–8).

5:19 Look at the claims of Jesus of Nazareth in verses 19–29 and ask yourself if these are the words of someone who was merely a "moral teacher": 1) He does what God does; 2) God shows Him all things; 3) As God raises the dead, Jesus raises whom He wills; 4) God has committed all judgment to Jesus; 5) Jesus said that all humanity should honor Him, just as they honor God; 6) Anyone who doesn't honor Jesus doesn't honor God; 7) Anyone who believes the words of Jesus has everlasting life; 8) Whoever trusts in Jesus is no longer condemned; 9) He has the life of God Himself; 10) The time will come when *billions* of dead people will hear the voice of Jesus and be raised from the dead by Him to stand in judgment.

The only sensible conclusion that we can come to is that Jesus was either completely deluded, a deceiver, or who He claimed to be—God in human form.

20 For the Father loves the Son, and shows him all things that he himself does: and he will show him greater works than these, that you may marvel.

21 For as the Father raises up the dead, and gives them life; even so the Son gives life to whom he will.

22 For the Father judges no man, but has committed all judgment to the Son:

23 That all men should honor the Son, even as they honor the Father. He who does not honor the Son does not honor the Father who has sent him.

24 Verily, verily, I say to you, He who hears my word and believes on him who sent me has everlasting life, and shall not come into condemnation; but has passed from death to life.

25 Verily, verily, I say to you, The hour is coming, and now is, when the dead shall hear the voice of the Son of God: and those who hear shall live.

26 For as the Father has life in himself; so has he given to the Son to have life in himself;

27 And has given him authority to execute judgment also, because he is the Son of man.

28 Do not marvel at this: for the hour is coming in which all who are in the graves shall hear his voice,

29 And shall come forth; those who have done good, to the resurrection of life; and those who have done evil, to the resurrection of damnation.

30 I can of myself do nothing: as I hear, I judge: and my judgment is just; because I do not seek my own will, but the will of the Father who has sent me.

31 If I bear witness of myself, my witness is not true.

32 There is another who bears witness of me; and I know that the witness which he witnesses of me is true.

• •

5:26 God is self-existent.

5:28 Jesus said, "The words that I speak to you are spirit, and they are life" (John 6:63). That's why He said very strange things about His voice. His voice (His words) brought Lazarus from the grave (John 11:43) and His voice will bring all the dead from their graves at the resurrection.

5:29 This time was also spoken of by the prophet Daniel: "Many of those who sleep in the dust of the earth shall awake, some to everlasting life, and some to shame and everlasting contempt" (Daniel 12:2).

33 You sent to John, and he bore witness to the truth.

34 But I do not receive testimony from man: but these things I say, that you might be saved.

35 He was a burning and a shining light: and you were willing for a season to rejoice in his light.

36 But I have greater witness than that of John: for the works which the Father has given me to finish, the same works that I do bear witness of me, that the Father has sent me.

37 And the Father himself, who has sent me, has borne witness of me. You have neither heard his voice at any time, nor seen his shape.

38 And you do not have his word abiding in you: for whom he has sent, him you do not believe.

39 Search the scriptures; for in them you think you have eternal life: and they are they which testify of me.

40 And you will not come to me, that you might have life.

41 I do not receive honor from men.

42 But I know you, that you do not have the love of God in you.

43 I have come in my Father's name, and you do not receive me: if another shall come in his own name, him you will receive.

44 How can you believe, who receive honor of one another, and do not seek the honor that comes from God only?

• •

5:36 John the Baptist never performed any miracles (see John 10:41). Jesus raised the dead, calmed a storm, turned water into wine, walked on water, and healed multitudes of sick people. His works showed that He had power over sickness, over the elements, and over death—proving that He was the Son of God, sent by the Father.

5:39 Jesus was saying that the whole of the Old Testament Scriptures speak of Him.

5:40 It isn't knowing Scripture, doing good deeds, or being religious that provides eternal life. It is available only in Jesus. Sinners must come to Him to have life: "God has given to us eternal life, and this life is in his Son. He who has the Son has life; and he who does not have the Son of God does not have life" (1 John 5:11,12).

Notice the word "will" in verse 40. It is not that sinners *cannot* be saved. It is that they *will* not: "The wicked, through the pride of his countenance, *will* not seek after God: God is in none of his thoughts" (Psalm 10:4, emphasis added).

5:44 The world is built on the foundation of honor from men. Men and women seek fame (honor from men) through music, sports, movies, etc.

45 Do not think that I will accuse you to the Father: there is one who accuses you, even Moses, in whom you trust.

46 For had you believed Moses, you would have believed me: for he wrote of me.

47 But if you do not believe his writings, how shall you believe my words?

• •

5:45   The Law of Moses stands as the accuser of sinful humanity. The religious leaders trusted in it for their salvation. However, the Law can't cleanse a man of his sin; it can only make him aware of it. That's its function—to act as a mirror to show us that we need God's mercy. The religious leaders didn't believe the Law of Moses (verse 46). They didn't like what they saw in the mirror, so they fogged it a little so that its reflection was more pleasing. Had  they believed the mirror, they would have run to the Savior for cleansing. Look at what Jesus said to them:

> "Well has Isaiah prophesied of you hypocrites, as it is written: This people honors me with their lips, but their heart is far from me. In vain do they worship me, teaching for doctrines the commandments of men. For laying aside the commandment of God, you hold the tradition of men, as the washing of pots and cups: and many other such things you do. Full well you reject the commandment of God, that you may keep your own tradition" (Mark 7:6–9).

CHAPTER 6

One of You is a Devil

A FTER these things Jesus went over the sea of Galilee, which is the sea of Tiberias.

2 And a great multitude followed him, because they saw his miracles which he did on those who were diseased.

3 And Jesus went up on a mountain, and there he sat with his disciples.

4 And the Passover, a feast of the Jews, was near.

5 When Jesus then lifted up his eyes, and saw a great company come to him, he said to Philip, Where shall we buy bread, that these may eat?

6 And this he said to prove him: for he himself knew what he would do.

7 Philip answered him, Two hundred pennyworth of bread is not sufficient for them, that every one of them may take a little.

8 One of his disciples, Andrew, Simon Peter's brother, said to him,

9 There is a lad here who has five barley loaves and two small fishes: but what are they among so many?

10 And Jesus said, Make the men sit down. Now there was much grass in the place. So the men sat down, in number about five thousand.

11 And Jesus took the loaves; and when he had given thanks, he distributed to the disciples, and the disciples to those who were sitting down; and likewise of the fishes as much as they wanted.

12 When they were filled, he said to his disciples, Gather up the fragments that remain, that nothing be lost.

13 Therefore they gathered them together, and filled twelve baskets with the fragments of the five barley loaves, which remained over and above by those who had eaten.

14 Then those men, when they had seen the miracle that Jesus did, said, This is truly that prophet who should come into the world.

15 When Jesus therefore perceived that they would come and take him by force, to make him a king, he departed again to a mountain by himself alone.

16 And when evening had come, his disciples went down to the sea,

17 And entered into a ship, and went over the sea toward Capernaum. And it was now dark, and Jesus had not come to them.

18 And the sea arose by reason of a great wind that blew.

19 So when they had rowed about twenty-five or thirty furlongs, they saw Jesus walking on the sea and drawing near to the ship: and they were afraid.

20 But he said to them, It is I; do not be afraid.

21 Then they willingly received him into the ship: and immediately the ship was at the land where they were going.

22 The following day, when the people who stood on the other side of the sea saw that there was no other boat there, except that one which his disciples had entered, and that Jesus had not gone with his disciples into the boat, but that his disciples had gone away alone;

23 (However other boats came from Tiberias near to the place where they ate bread after the Lord had given thanks:)

24 When the people therefore saw that Jesus was not there, nor

• •

6:14   Moses wrote of the Prophet that God would send: "I will raise them up a Prophet from among their brethren, like you, and will put my words in his mouth; and he shall speak to them all that I shall command him" (Deuteronomy 18:18).

6:15   Jesus didn't come to be made a king. He came to earth to die for the sins of mankind so we could inherit heaven. In the same way, don't be tempted to settle for temporary pleasures when you could have eternal life.

6:19   This distance was three or four miles. It is no big thing for the Creator to have dominion over His creation. The time will come when He will exercise His dominion over all of humanity. Give it to Him in the Day of His grace, before He takes it in the Day of His wrath.

his disciples, they also got into boats and came to Capernaum, seeking Jesus.

25 And when they had found him on the other side of the sea, they said to him, Rabbi, when did you come here?

26 Jesus answered them and said, Verily, verily, I say to you, You seek me, not because you saw the miracles, but because you ate of the loaves and were filled.

27 Do not labor for the food which perishes, but for that food which endures to everlasting life, which the Son of man shall give to you: for God the Father has sealed him.

28 Then they said to him, What shall we do, that we might work the works of God?

29 Jesus answered and said to them, This is the work of God, that you believe on him whom he has sent.

30 They therefore said to him, What sign do you show then, that we may see and believe you? what do you work?

31 Our fathers ate manna in the desert; as it is written, He gave them bread from heaven to eat.

32 Then Jesus said to them, Verily, verily, I say to you, Moses did

• •

6:27 One of the greatest revelations any of us can have is that everything outside the kingdom of God is futile. This is because it is temporal; this life is perishing. Have you ever given deep thought to the question, "What am I 'laboring' for?" These sobering words from cartoonist Ralph Barton reveal perhaps the greatest reason people choose to take their lives. His suicide note said, "I have had few difficulties, many friends, great success . . . but I am fed up with inventing devices to fill up 24 hours of the day." He was insightful enough to see that this life (pleasure though it has) is futile. The great Russian novelist Leo Tolstoy said, "What is life for? To die? To kill myself at once? No, I am afraid. To wait for death until it comes? I fear that even more. Then I must live. But what for? In order to die? And I could not escape from that circle." Jesus Christ destroyed that "circle." When true conversion takes place, death loses its sting. Life is no longer futile.

6:29 Most religions teach that certain works are required in order to be saved. Here God tells us the only "work" He considers: "believe on him whom he has sent." Jesus is again speaking of Himself.

6:31 Manna was the Israelites' chief food during their 40 years in the wilderness (Exodus 16:15,35). When Israel grumbled at the lack of food in the wilderness of Sin, God gave them 'bread from heaven' (Exodus 16:3,4; Psalm 78:23,24), and His provision did not cease until they crossed into Canaan and ate the food of that land (Joshua 5:12), despite their grumbling.

not give you that bread from heaven; but my Father gives you the true bread from heaven.

33 For the bread of God is he who came down from heaven, and gives life to the world.

34 Then they said to him, Lord, evermore give us this bread.

35 And Jesus said to them, I am the bread of life: he who comes to me shall never hunger; and he who believes on me shall never thirst.

36 But I said to you, That you also have seen me, and do not believe.

37 All whom the Father gives me shall come to me; and he who comes to me I will by no means cast out.

38 For I came down from heaven, not to do my own will, but the will of him who sent me.

39 And this is the will of the Father who has sent me, that of all he has given me I should lose nothing, but should raise it up again at the last day.

40 And this is the will of him who sent me, that everyone who sees the Son, and believes on him, may have everlasting life: and I will raise him up at the last day.

41 The Jews then murmured at him, because he said, I am the bread which came down from heaven.

42 And they said, Is this not Jesus, the son of Joseph, whose father and mother we know? how is it then that he says, I came down from heaven?

43 Jesus therefore answered and said to them, Do not murmur among yourselves.

44 No man can come to me unless the Father who has sent me

• •

6:35 Bread is the staple of this life on earth. Jesus calls Himself the staple of eternal life.

6:37 Here is a wonderful open-ended promise. It doesn't matter what shameful deeds we have done or thoughts we have had, we will be accepted by the Savior—if we come on His terms.

6:38 Jesus was preexistent: "Jesus Christ the same yesterday, and today, and forever" (Hebrews 13:8).

6:41 It is understandable that they were offended by someone who kept saying, "I came down from heaven." However, had they believed the Old Testament Scriptures, they would have recognized Jesus of Nazareth as the Messiah. There are more than 300 prophecies related to His coming.

draws him: and I will raise him up at the last day.

45 It is written in the prophets, And they shall all be taught by God. Every man therefore who has heard, and has learned from the Father, comes to me.

46 Not that any man has seen the Father, except he who is of God, he has seen the Father.

47 Verily, verily, I say to you, He who believes on me has everlasting life.

• •

6:44   The reason you can read these verses with an open heart is that God is drawing you to Himself. The very impulse we have to seek Him comes from His gracious hand. There is nothing in us that desires the God revealed in the Bible. We *run* from the light, if He is not drawing us to Himself. Just as nothing in us causes the life-giving sun to shine its rays upon us, so the grace that causes God to shine His love upon us doesn't come from some virtue in us. It radiates from God to us because God is love.

6:46   Jesus preexisted as part of the Godhead: "But we see Jesus, who was made a little lower than the angels for the suffering of death, crowned with glory and honor; that by the grace of God he should taste death for every man" (Hebrews 2:9). Colossians 2:8,9 says, "Beware lest any man spoil you through philosophy and vain deceit, after the tradition of men, after the rudiments of the world, and not after Christ. *For in him dwells all the fullness of the Godhead bodily*" (emphasis added).

6:47   The moment a sinner repents and trusts the Savior, he *has* eternal life. Do you "believe on" Jesus? Are you *trusting* Him for your eternal salvation? You do this by repenting and placing your faith in Him. Repentance involves confessing your sins (agreeing with God that they are sins) and turning from them. If there was one chance in a million that Jesus of Nazareth is who He claimed to be—that He abolished death, as the Bible says—then you owe it to your good sense to at least look into it. You have nothing to lose. The way to see if you need the Savior is to look for a moment at the Ten Commandments. Let's look into the mirror of God's Law.

Have you ever lied (even once—fibs, white lies, etc.)? Have you ever stolen anything (the value is irrelevant)? Jesus said, "Whoever looks upon a woman to lust after her, has committed adultery already with her in his heart." Have you ever looked with lust? If you have said "Yes" to these three questions, by your own admission, you are a lying, thieving, adulterer at heart; and we've only looked at three of the Ten Commandments. Have you put God first in your life? Is He the focal point of your affections? Or have you created a god to suit yourself, a god with whom you feel comfortable? This is called "idolatry," and the Bible warns that idolaters will not inherit the kingdom of God (1 Corinthians 6:9,10). Have you ever used God's holy name in vain? Have you kept the Sabbath holy? Have you always honored your parents? Have you ever been

48 I am that bread of life.

49 Your fathers ate manna in the wilderness, and are dead.

50 This is the bread which came down from heaven, that a man may eat of it and not die.

51 I am the living bread which came down from heaven: if any man eats of this bread, he shall live forever: and the bread that I will give is my flesh, which I will give for the life of the world.

52 The Jews therefore argued among themselves, saying, How can this man give us his flesh to eat?

53 Then Jesus said to them, Verily, verily, I say to you, Except you eat the flesh of the Son of man, and drink his blood, you have no life in you.

54 Whoever eats my flesh, and drinks my blood, has eternal life;

• •

guilty of wanting something that belonged to someone else?

Listen to your conscience, the impartial judge in the courtroom of your mind, and answer this question: If God judges you by the Ten Commandments, will you be innocent or guilty on the Day of Judgment? You know that you will be guilty, and therefore end up in hell. That's not God's will. He provided a way for you to be forgiven. He sent His Son to take your punishment: "God commends His love toward us, in that, while we were yet sinners, Christ died for us" (Romans 5:8). He was bruised for our iniquities. We broke God's Law, and Jesus paid our fine. Then He rose from the dead and defeated death.

The following words were spoken in prayer to God by King David, when he realized that he had sinned against Him by committing adultery and murder. Perhaps you could make them your prayer:

> "Have mercy upon me, O God, according to your lovingkindness: according to the multitude of your tender mercies, blot out my transgressions. Wash me thoroughly from my iniquity, and cleanse me from my sin. For I acknowledge my transgressions: and my sin is ever before me. Against you, you only, have I sinned, and done this evil in your sight: that you might be justified when you speak, and be blameless when you judge. Behold, I was shaped in iniquity; and in sin my mother conceived me. Behold, you desire truth in the inward parts: and in the hidden part you shall make me to know wisdom. Purge me with hyssop, and I shall be clean: wash me, and I shall be whiter than snow. Make me to hear joy and gladness, that the bones which you have broken may rejoice. Hide your face from my sins, and blot out all my iniquities. Create in me a clean heart, O God; and renew a right spirit within me" (Psalm 51:1–10).

If you prayed that prayer, you may like to turn to the back of this book and begin reading "Principles of Christian Growth."

and I will raise him up at the last day.

55 For my flesh is food indeed, and my blood is drink indeed.

56 He who eats my flesh, and drinks my blood, dwells in me, and I in him.

57 As the living Father has sent me, and I live by the Father: so he who eats me, even he shall live by me.

58 This is that bread which came down from heaven: not as your fathers ate manna and are dead: he who eats of this bread shall live forever.

59 These things he said in the synagogue, as he taught in Capernaum.

60 Therefore many of his disciples, when they had heard this, said, This is a hard saying; who can hear it?

61 When Jesus knew in himself that his disciples murmured at it, he said to them, Does this offend you?

62 What then if you shall see the Son of man ascend where he was before?

63 It is the Spirit who gives life; the flesh profits nothing: the words that I speak to you are spirit, and they are life.

- -

6:51 Jesus here starts a course of conversation that seems to be bizarre, weird, peculiar, strange, and fantastic (in the truest sense of the word). It leaves no ground for the "Jesus was a great teacher" viewpoint. He speaks of people eating His flesh and drinking His blood, something utterly repulsive, if taken literally. It is equivalent to a religious teacher saying that His followers must eat his liver. No wonder those who heard Him were offended. Jesus then qualifies His words by saying, "What then if you shall see the Son of man ascend to where He was before?" (verse 62). In other words, would they still be offended if they saw Jesus bodily rise up into the heavens? (This was something His disciples actually witnessed—see Acts 1:9.) If Jesus proved Himself to be God by physically ascending into the heavens, then they had better listen without offense.

If someone wants to find something offensive in the Bible, there is plenty that can rub them the wrong way. However, when religious leaders were affronted because Jesus had cast out a demon, He answered, "But if I cast out devils with the finger of God, no doubt the kingdom of God has come upon you" (Luke 11:20). In other words, if something Jesus said rubs the fur the wrong way, let the cat turn around. Get rid of your offense because the power of Almighty God stands behind the Savior. The mention of drinking blood and eating flesh is repulsive; however, faith says, "This makes no sense to me, but I trust God." That's the first principle of faith in God.

64 But there are some of you who do not believe. For Jesus knew from the beginning who they were who did not believe, and who should betray him.

65 And he said, Therefore I said to you that no man can come to me, unless it has been granted to him by my Father.

66 From that time many of his disciples went back, and walked with him no more.

67 Then Jesus said to the twelve, Will you also go away?

68 Then Simon Peter answered him, Lord, to whom shall we go? you have the words of eternal life.

69 And we believe and are sure that you are that Christ, the Son of the living God.

70 Jesus answered them, Have I not chosen you twelve, and one of you is a devil?

71 He spoke of Judas Iscariot the son of Simon: for it was he who should betray him, being one of the twelve.

• •

6:63   Jesus explained that His words were *spiritual* statements. Salvation doesn't come through eating bread and drinking wine. It comes through the reality of the psalmist's admission: "O taste and see that the LORD is good: blessed is the man who trusts in him!" (Psalm 34:8). Salvation comes through partaking of Jesus Christ *spiritually*. This occurs the moment we are born again. Sadly, millions trust in bread and wine thinking that their physical presence in the body provides salvation, when it is the presence of Jesus Christ in the believer, through the Holy Spirit, that is the promise and source of life. That's why the Bible says, "He who believes on the Son has everlasting life: and he who does not believe the Son shall not see life; but the wrath of God abides on him" (John 3:36).

6:68   Jesus of Nazareth alone has the words of eternal life. Look at the sayings of any of history's great religious leaders and you will discover that they were mere men. They may have had charisma, and their words may have been insightful. But they were just men, subject to the weaknesses of humanity. Napoleon Bonaparte said, "I know men and I tell you that Jesus Christ is no mere man. Between Him and every other person in the world there is no possible term of comparison. Alexander, Caesar, Charlemagne, and I have founded empires. But on what did we rest the creations of our genius? Upon force. Jesus Christ founded His empire upon love; and at this hour millions of men would die for Him." Jesus is no mere man. He is the King of kings and the Lord of all lords.

CHAPTER 7

Why Do You Seek to Kill Me?

A FTER these things Jesus walked in Galilee: for he would not walk in Judea, because the Jews sought to kill him.

2 Now the Jews' feast of tabernacles was at hand.

3 His brethren therefore said to him, Depart from here and go into Judea, that your disciples also may see the works that you do.

4 For there is no man who does anything in secret, and he himself seeks to be known openly. If you do these things, show yourself to the world.

5 For neither did his brethren believe in him.

6 Then Jesus said to them, My time has not yet come: but your time is always ready.

7 The world cannot hate you; but it hates me, because I testify of it, that its works are evil.

8 Go up to this feast: I am not yet going up to this feast; for my time has not yet fully come.

9 When he had said these words to them, he remained in Galilee.

· ·

7:5 Jesus had brothers and sisters. After He was born, Mary had other children, and therefore should no longer be referred to as the *virgin* Mary: "Is this not the carpenter's son? is not his mother called Mary? and his brethren, James, and Joses, and Simon, and Judas? and his sisters, are they not all with us?" (Matthew 13:55,56).

7:7 The world hates Jesus Christ. How many other great historical figures have their name used as a cuss word? The reason they hate Him is because His words accuse them of evil. They hate Him for the same reason criminals hate those who enforce the law.

7:8 This is another reference to His upcoming death on the cross.

10 But when his brethren had gone up, then he also went up to the feast, not openly, but as it were in secret.

11 Then the Jews sought him at the feast, and said, Where is he?

12 And there was much murmuring among the people concerning him: for some said, He is a good man: others said, No; but he deceives the people.

13 However, no man spoke openly of him for fear of the Jews.

14 Now about the midst of the feast Jesus went up into the temple, and taught.

15 And the Jews marveled, saying, How does this man know letters, having never learned?

16 Jesus answered them, and said, My doctrine is not mine, but his who sent me.

17 If any man will do his will, he shall know of the doctrine, whether it be of God, or whether I speak of myself.

18 He who speaks of himself seeks his own glory: but he who seeks the glory of him who sent him, the same is true, and no unrighteousness is in him.

19 Did not Moses give you the law, and yet none of you keeps the law? Why do you go about to kill me?

20 The people answered and said, You have a devil: who goes about to kill you?

21 Jesus answered and said to them, I have done one work, and you all marvel.

22 Moses therefore gave to you circumcision (not because it is of Moses, but of the fathers); and you circumcise a man on the Sabbath day.

23 If a man on the Sabbath day receives circumcision, that the law of Moses should not be broken, are you angry at me, because

· ·

7:17 This is the universal challenge to humanity. If *any man* does the will of God he will come to know that Jesus of Nazareth is the Messiah—the Door that leads to immortality, the only antidote to death. What then is the will of God? See John 6:29.

7:19 None of us has kept the Law of God. It wasn't given so we could earn salvation by keeping it, but so we could know what sin is. A mirror can't cleanse. Its function is to show us that we are unclean. Do you dare look into the mirror? It will reveal what is, and what will be.

7:20 See verse 25.

I have made a man completely whole on the Sabbath day?

24 Do not judge according to the appearance, but judge with righteous judgment.

25 Then some of them of Jerusalem said, Is this not he whom they seek to kill?

26 But, look, he speaks boldly, and they say nothing to him. Do the rulers know indeed that this is the very Christ?

27 However, we know where this man is from: but when Christ comes, no man knows where he is from.

28 Then Jesus cried in the temple as he taught, saying, You both know me, and you know where I am from: and I have not come of myself, but he who sent me is true, whom you do not know.

29 But I know him: for I am from him, and he has sent me.

30 Then they sought to take him: but no man laid hands on him, because his hour had not yet come.

31 And many of the people believed on him, and said, When Christ comes, will he do more miracles than these which this man has done?

32 The Pharisees heard that the people murmured such things concerning him; and the Pharisees and the chief priests sent officers to take him.

33 Then Jesus said to them, Yet a little while I shall be with you, and then I go to him who sent me.

34 You shall seek me, and shall not find me: and where I am, there you cannot come.

35 Then the Jews said among themselves, Where will he go, that we shall not find him? will he go to the dispersed among the Gentiles, and teach the Gentiles?

36 What manner of saying is this that he said, You shall seek me, and shall not find me: and where I am, there you cannot come?

37 In the last day, that great day of the feast, Jesus stood and cried, saying, If any man thirsts, let him come to me and drink.

38 He who believes on me, as the scripture has said, out of his

• •

7:24 When Christians speak of sin, the world is often quick to quote the words of Jesus, "Judge not, that you be not judged." However, in the context of that verse, Jesus is not saying that Christians don't have the liberty to make moral judgments. He is actually saying to *Christians* that they shouldn't judge one another (see Matthew 7:1–5 and note the word "brother").

7:30 This is another reference to His upcoming death on the cross.

heart shall flow rivers of living water.

39 (But this he spoke of the Spirit, whom those who believe on him should receive: for the Holy Spirit was not yet given; because Jesus was not yet glorified.)

40 Many of the people therefore, when they heard this saying, said, Truly this is the Prophet.

41 Others said, This is the Christ. But some said, Shall Christ come out of Galilee?

42 Has not the scripture said, That Christ comes of the seed of David, and out of the town of Bethlehem, where David was?

43 So there was a division among the people because of him.

44 And some of them would have taken him; but no man laid

• •

7:37   Are you thirsting for righteousness? If you are a normal human being, you will have little or no desire for it. Understandably, it is the *pleasures* of sin for which you thirst. What then would make any person desire righteousness? It is the knowledge that without it, you will perish: "Riches do not profit in the day of wrath: but righteousness delivers from death" (Proverbs 11:4). This is what Jesus said about "righteousness": "Blessed are those who hunger  and thirst after righteousness: for they shall be filled . . . For I say to you, That except your righteousness shall exceed the righteousness of the scribes and Pharisees, you shall in no case enter into the kingdom of heaven" (Matthew 5:6; 5:20). To be righteous in the sight of God, you must be perfect, in thought, word, and deed (Matthew 5:48). Since none of us is perfect, the only way we can be considered righteous is to place our trust in Christ: "For he has made him who knew no sin to be sin for us, that we might be made the righteousness of God in him" (2 Corinthians 5:21).

7:40   See comment at John 6:14.

7:42   If these folks had had the good sense to inquire, they would have found that Jesus *did* come out of Bethlehem. This is often the case with skeptics. They will accuse God of being double-minded by saying that He commands, "You shall not kill," and yet demands "an eye for an eye." However, if they inquired, they would find that the Sixth Commandment is directed to all humanity; it outlaws murder. "An eye for an eye" is God's directive for proceedings when civil or moral Law is broken. We call it "restitution." If someone takes your car, they should pay back a car—car for car, eye for eye, tooth for tooth, life for life. If skeptics were really seeking the truth, they should look a little further than their own prejudices. However, most are not seeking truth, but excuses to justify remaining in their sins.

hands on him.

45 Then the officers came to the chief priests and Pharisees; and they said to them, Why have you not brought him?

46 The officers answered, No man ever spoke like this man.

47 Then the Pharisees answered them, Are you also deceived?

48 Have any of the rulers or of the Pharisees believed on him?

49 But this people who do not know the law are cursed.

50 Nicodemus (he who came to Jesus by night, being one of them) said to them,

51 Does our law judge any man before it hears him and knows what he does?

52 They answered and said to him, Are you also of Galilee? Search, and look: for no prophet arises out of Galilee.

53 And every man went to his own house.

· ·

7:46 The officers were sent to arrest Jesus and were instead themselves arrested by His incredible words. How true was their own confession: "No man ever spoke like this man." Look at these amazing words spoken by Jesus to His hearers: "Blessed are your eyes, for they see: and your ears, for they hear. For verily I say to you, That many prophets and righteous men have desired to see those things which you see, and have not seen them; and to hear those things which you hear, and have not heard them" (Matthew 13:16,17). He was speaking of Himself. He also said, "He who loves father or mother more than me is not worthy of me: and he who loves son or daughter more than me is not worthy of me" (Matthew 10:37). Either this was the greatest egotist who ever lived, or this was the very source of life in human form.

Even trembling demons bowed to His Lordship: "In the synagogue there was a man who had a spirit of an unclean devil, and cried out with a loud voice, saying, Let us alone; what have we to do with you, Jesus of Nazareth? Did you come to destroy us? I know you, who you are; the Holy One of God. And Jesus rebuked him, saying, Hold your peace, and come out of him. And when the devil had thrown him in the midst, he came out of him, and did not hurt him" (Luke 4:33–35).

7:52 See verse 42 comment.

CHAPTER 8

Caught in Adultery

JESUS went to the Mount of Olives.

2 And early in the morning he came again into the temple, and all the people came to him; and he sat down and taught them.

3 And the scribes and Pharisees brought to him a woman taken in adultery; and when they had set her in the midst,

4 They said to him, Master, this woman was taken in adultery, in the very act.

5 Now Moses in the law commanded us that such should be stoned: but what do you say?

• •

8:3   Man brings much of the world's woes upon himself by his own sin. Consider the way dogs cross the road. A dog will wander onto a freeway oblivious to the danger. His tail wags as he steps between cars without a second thought. Cars swerve. Tires squeal. The noise is deafening as vehicles smash into each other. The sleepy dog stops wagging his tail for a moment and looks at the pile of smoldering, broken cars on the freeway. His expression betrays his thoughts. His bone-burying brain doesn't realize for one moment that he is responsible for the disaster.

When man wanders onto the freeway of sin, his tail wags with delight. He thinks that this is what he was made for. His thoughts of any repercussions for his actions are shallow. His mind wanders into lust, then predictably he wanders onto the path of adultery. Suddenly a disaster sits before him. His marriage is shattered, his name is slurred, and his children are twisted and scarred. But like the dumb dog, he doesn't realize for one moment that he is solely responsible for the disaster by his sin.

8:4   You too have been caught in the very act of sin. God is a witness to every evil deed, and He will bring every work to judgment, including every secret thing, whether it is good or evil.

8:5   Their strategy was to have Him compromise the Law by showing mercy to this guilty woman. However, He was able to extend forgiveness because He

6 This they said, tempting him, that they might have to accuse him. But Jesus stooped down, and with his finger wrote on the ground, as though he had not heard them.

7 So when they continued asking him, he lifted himself up and said to them, He who is without sin among you, let him cast a stone at her first.

8 And again he stooped down, and wrote on the ground.

9 And those who heard it, being convicted by their own conscience, went out one by one, beginning at the eldest, even to the last: and Jesus was left alone, and the woman standing in the midst.

10 When Jesus had lifted himself up and saw none but the woman, he said to her, Woman, where are your accusers? has no man condemned you?

11 She said, No man, Lord. And Jesus said to her, Neither do I condemn you: go, and sin no more.

12 Then Jesus spoke again to them, saying, I am the light of the

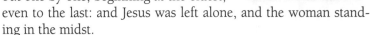

was on His way to suffer on the cross for her sins and the sin of the world, that the Law of God might be honored.

8:7 He was the only One without sin.

8:9 Perhaps Jesus wrote the Ten Commandments on the ground. What else does God write with His finger? (See Exodus 31:18.) The work of the Law was written on the hearts of His hearers (see Romans 2:15), and they left one by one as their conscience did its accusatory duty, boldly verifying the truth of each Commandment. The Law strips us of our holier-than-thou self-righteousness. We dare not point a finger at another when the ten condemning fingers of a holy Creator are pointed at us. It was the Law that brought the sinful woman to the feet of Jesus. It left her with no other option than to run from its wrath to the Savior. That's its function. The Law sends us to Jesus for mercy.

8:11 The same Law that called for the blood of this sinful woman also calls for your blood. You have the same choice as this woman. You can face the merciless wrath of the Law and spend eternity in hell, or you can repent of your sins, fall at the feet of Jesus Christ, and trust in His blood and His wonderful mercy to save you. She was saved because Jesus was *going* to the cross; you can be saved because He *went* to the cross.

world: he who follows me shall not walk in darkness, but shall have the light of life.

13 The Pharisees therefore said to him, You bear record of yourself; your record is not true.

14 Jesus answered and said to them, Though I bear record of myself, yet my record is true: for I know where I came from, and where I go; but you cannot tell where I come from, and where I go.

15 You judge after the flesh; I judge no man.

16 And yet if I judge, my judgment is true: for I am not alone, but I am with the Father who sent me.

17 It is also written in your law, that the testimony of two men is true.

18 I am one who bears witness of myself, and the Father who sent me bears witness of me.

19 Then they said to him, Where is your Father? Jesus answered, You neither know me, nor my Father: if you had known me, you should have known my Father also.

20 These words Jesus spoke in the treasury, as he taught in the temple: and no man laid hands on him; for his hour had not yet come.

21 Then Jesus said again to them, I go my way, and you shall seek me, and shall die in your sins: where I go, you cannot come.

22 Then the Jews said, Will he kill himself? because he says, Where I go, you cannot come.

23 And he said to them, You are from beneath; I am from above:

• •

8:11   Someone who truly repents stops sinning *willfully*. The Christian may *fall* into sin, but it against his will (it grieves him), and he immediately seeks God for mercy. See 1 John 1:9.

8:16   The thought may have entered your mind that perhaps God will *overlook* your sins. Perhaps He, in His mercy, could just look the other way. If He does so, then He is unjust. Think of it in connection with civil law. Can a judge look the other way when a criminal is obviously guilty, and be true to what is right? Even if the judge feels sorry for the criminal, he must stay true to the law. Justice must be done. During the 1980s in the U.S., more than 60,000 murders were committed in which the murderers got away totally free. No doubt the figure is higher, as many "accidents" and "suicides" are actually murders in disguise. These are people who have raped, tortured, and strangled helpless victims. Should God overlook their crimes on Judgment Day? Should He turn a blind eye? Should He compromise Eternal Justice?

8:20   This is another reference to the cross.

you are of this world; I am not of this world.

24 I therefore said to you, that you shall die in your sins: for if you do not believe that I am he, you shall die in your sins.

25 Then they said to him, Who are you? And Jesus said to them, Even the same that I said to you from the beginning.

26 I have many things to say and to judge of you: but he who sent me is true; and I speak to the world those things which I have heard of him.

27 They did not understand that he spoke to them of the Father.

28 Then Jesus said to them, When you have lifted up the Son of man, then you shall know that I am he, and that I do nothing of myself; but as my Father has taught me, I speak these things.

29 And he who sent me is with me: the Father has not left me alone; for I always do those things that please him.

30 As he spoke these words, many believed on him.

31 Then Jesus said to those Jews who believed on him, If you continue in my word, then you are my disciples indeed;

32 And you shall know the truth, and the truth shall make you free.

33 They answered him, We are Abraham's seed, and were never in bondage to any man: how do you say, You shall be made free?

34 Jesus answered them, Verily, verily, I say to you, Whoever commits sin is the servant of sin.

· ·

8:24 It would be better for you not to have been born than for you to die in your sins and spend eternity in hell.

8:25 They knew that this was Jesus "the carpenter's son," but His words were so strange that they were aware this was no ordinary man.

8:28 This is another reference to the cross of Calvary, the purpose for which He came to earth. See John 3:14 comment.

8:29 These are the things that please God: Jesus fulfilled the whole Law of God. He never sinned once. He loved the Father with all of His heart, mind, soul, and strength (proven by His obedience to God in going to the cross), and He loved His neighbor as Himself (proven by His going to the cross for us).

8:34 The world throws off the chains of restraint. They think that they are free to drink as much alcohol as they desire; to eat to the full, gamble, smoke, read pornography, and express any emotion that comes their way without any consequences. At the same time, we have special programs for multitudes who have found themselves to be slaves to gambling, smoking, alcohol, drugs, anger, greed, guilt, pornography, and obesity.

35 And the servant does not abide in the house forever: but the Son abides forever.

36 Therefore if the Son shall make you free, you shall be free indeed.

37 I know that you are Abraham's seed; but you seek to kill me, because my word has no place in you.

38 I speak that which I have seen with my Father: and you do that which you have seen with your father.

39 They answered and said to him, Abraham is our father. Jesus said to them, If you were Abraham's children, you would do the works of Abraham.

40 But now you seek to kill me, a man who has told you the truth, which I have heard of God: Abraham did not do this.

41 You do the deeds of your father. Then they said to him, We were not born of fornication; we have one Father, even God.

42 Jesus said to them, If God were your Father, you would love me: for I proceeded forth and came from God; neither have I come of myself, but he sent me.

43 Why do you not understand my speech? even because you cannot hear my word.

44 You are of your father the devil, and the lusts of your father you will do. He was a murderer from the beginning, and did not abide in the truth, because there is no truth in him. When he speaks a lie, he speaks of his own: for he is a liar, and the father of it.

45 And because I tell you the truth, you do not believe me.

46 Which of you convicts me of sin? And if I say the truth, why do you not believe me?

47 He who is of God hears God's words: therefore you do not hear them, because you are not of God.

48 Then the Jews answered and said to him, Do we not say well

· ·

8:44 We are not all "children of God," as some think. Until we are born into God's family through the new birth (John 3:3), our spiritual father is the devil. We are born with *his* image and likeness. Anger, hate, greed, selfishness, lust, deceit, jealousy, pride, envy, etc., are traits that come naturally to each of us.

8:46 Jesus was without sin. The Bible says that He "knew no sin" (2 Corinthians 5:21), that He was "in all points tempted as we are, yet without sin" (Hebrews 4:15), and that He "committed no sin, nor was guile found in His mouth" (1 Peter 2:22).

that you are a Samaritan, and have a devil?

49 Jesus answered, I do not have a devil; but I honor my Father, and you do dishonor me.

50 And I do not seek my own glory: there is one who seeks and judges.

51 Verily, verily, I say to you, If a man keeps my saying, he shall never see death.

52 Then the Jews said to him, Now we know that you have a devil. Abraham is dead, and the prophets; and you say, If a man keeps my saying, he shall never see death.

53 Are you greater than our father Abraham, who is dead? and the prophets are dead: whom do you make yourself?

54 Jesus answered, If I honor myself, my honor is nothing: it is my Father who honors me; of whom you say that he is your God:

55 Yet you have not known him; but I know him: and if I should say, I do not know him, I shall be a liar like you: but I know him, and keep his saying.

56 Your father Abraham rejoiced to see my day: and he saw it and was glad.

57 Then the Jews said to him, You are not yet fifty years old, and you have seen Abraham?

58 Jesus said to them, Verily, verily, I say to you, Before Abraham was, I am.

59 Then they took up stones to cast at him: but Jesus hid himself, and went out of the temple, going through the midst of them, and so passed by.

· ·

8:48 The religious leaders were trying to *demonize* Him.

8:51   No religious teacher has ever dared say such a thing. Only God could make this claim.

8:56   Abraham had faith that God would send the Messiah and liberate humanity from death. (See Hebrews 11:8–13.)

8:58   When Moses asked God who he should say had sent him to lead Israel out of Egypt, the Bible says, "God said to Moses, I AM WHO I AM: and he said, Thus you shall say to the children of Israel, I AM has sent me to you" (Exodus 3:14). The name "I AM" reveals that God is eternal. Time is a dimension that He created and to which He subjected man, but God Himself dwells in *eternity*, outside the dimension of time. God isn't "I WAS" or "I WILL BE." He IS. Jesus claimed this name of God for Himself, which was considered the epitome of blasphemy.

CHAPTER 9

Born Blind

A ND as Jesus passed by, he saw a man who was blind from his birth.

2 And his disciples asked him, saying, Master, who did sin, this man or his parents, that he was born blind?

• •

9:1 Until we come to the Savior, we too are blind from birth. The Bible tells us that the god of this world (Satan) has blinded the minds of those who do not believe (2 Corinthians 4:4).

9:2 Why Is There Suffering? Some may ask why God would create a man without the ability to see. Others have wondered why there is suffering, pain, and death. Skeptics even use this point to try to prove that there is no God, or at least no God who is benevolent. ("If God is a God of love, why does He let people suffer?") While the reason God allows suffering may be difficult to understand, the existence of suffering is obvious. Study the soil for a moment. It naturally produces weeds. No one plants them; no one waters them. They even stubbornly push through cracks of a dry sidewalk. Millions of useless weeds sprout like there's no tomorrow, strangling our crops and ruining our lawns. Pull them out by the roots, and there will be more tomorrow. They are nothing but a curse!

Consider how much of the earth is uninhabitable. There are millions of square miles of barren deserts in Africa and other parts of the world. Most of Australia is nothing but miles and miles of useless desolate land. Not only that, but the earth is constantly shaken with massive earthquakes. Its shores are lashed with hurricanes; tornadoes rip through creation with incredible fury; devastating floods soak the land; and terrible droughts parch the soil. The earth's inhabitants are afflicted with disease, pain, suffering, and death. Think of how many people are plagued with cancer, Alzheimer's, multiple sclerosis, heart disease, emphysema, Parkinson's, and a number of other debilitating illnesses. Consider all the children with leukemia, or people born with crippling diseases or without the mental capability to even feed themselves. All these things should convince thinking minds that something is radically wrong. *Did*

3 Jesus answered, Neither has this man sinned, nor his parents: but that the works of God should be made manifest in him.

4 I must work the works of him who sent me, while it is day: the night comes, when no man can work.

5 As long as I am in the world, I am the light of the world.

6 When he had thus spoken, he spat on the ground, and made clay of the spittle, and he anointed the eyes of the blind man with

. . . .

God blow it when He created humanity? What sort of tyrant must our Creator be if this was His master plan?

Sadly, many use the issue of suffering as an excuse to reject any thought of God, when its existence is the *very reason* we should accept Him. Suffering stands as terrible testimony to the truth of the explanation given by the Word of God. But how can we know that the Bible is true? Simply by studying the prophecies of Matthew 24, Luke 21, and 2 Timothy 3. A few minutes of open-hearted inspection will convince any honest skeptic that this is no ordinary book. It is the supernatural testament of our Creator about why there is suffering . . . and what we can do about it. The Bible tells us that God cursed the earth because of Adam's transgression. Weeds *are* a curse. So is disease. Sin and suffering cannot be separated. The Scriptures inform us that we live in a *fallen* creation. In the beginning, God created man perfect, and he lived in a perfect world without suffering. *It was heaven on earth*. When sin came into the world, death and misery came with it.

Those who understand the message of Holy Scripture eagerly await a new heaven and a new earth "in which righteousness dwells." In that coming kingdom there will be no more pain, suffering, disease, or death. We are told that no eye has ever seen, nor has any ear heard, neither has any man's mind ever imagined the wonderful things that God has in store for those who love Him (1 Corinthians 2:9). Think for a moment what it would be like if food grew with the fervor of weeds. Consider how wonderful it would be if the deserts became incredibly fertile, if creation stopped devouring humanity. Imagine if the weather worked *for* us instead of against us, if disease completely disappeared, if pain was a thing of the past, if death was no more.

The dilemma is that we are like a child whose insatiable appetite for chocolate has caused his face to break out with ugly sores. He looks in the mirror and sees a sight that makes him depressed. But instead of giving up his beloved chocolate, he consoles himself by stuffing more into his mouth. Yet, the source of his pleasure is actually the *cause* of his suffering. The whole face of the earth is nothing but ugly sores of suffering. Everywhere we look we see unspeakable pain. But instead of believing God's explanation and asking Him to forgive us and change our appetite, we run deeper into sin's sweet embrace. There we find solace in its temporal pleasures, thus intensifying our pain, both in this life and in the life to come.

the clay,

7 And said to him, Go, wash in the pool of Siloam (which is by interpretation, Sent). Therefore he went his way and washed, and came back seeing.

8 Therefore the neighbors, and those who before had seen him who was blind, said, Is this not he who sat and begged?

9 Some said, This is he: others said, He is like him: but he said, I am he.

10 Therefore they said to him, How were your eyes opened?

11 He answered and said, A man who is called Jesus made clay and anointed my eyes, and said to me, Go to the pool of Siloam, and wash: and I went and washed, and I received sight.

12 Then they said to him, Where is he? He said, I do not know.

13 They brought to the Pharisees him who formerly was blind.

14 And it was the Sabbath day when Jesus made the clay, and opened his eyes.

15 Then again the Pharisees also asked him how he had received his sight. He said to them, He put clay upon my eyes, and I washed, and do see.

16 Therefore some of the Pharisees said, This man is not of God, because he does not keep the Sabbath day. Others said, How can a man who is a sinner do such miracles? And there was a division among them.

17 They said to the blind man again, What do you say of him who has opened your eyes? He said, He is a prophet.

18 But the Jews did not believe concerning him, that he had been blind and received his sight, until they called the parents of him who had received his sight.

19 And they asked them, saying, Is this your son, who you say was born blind? how then does he now see?

20 His parents answered them and said, We know that this is our son, and that he was born blind:

21 But by what means he now sees, we do not know; or who has opened his eyes, we do not know: he is of age; ask him: he shall speak for himself.

22 His parents spoke these words because they feared the Jews: for the Jews had agreed already that if any man did confess that he was Christ, he should be put out of the synagogue.

23 Therefore his parents said, He is of age; ask him.

24 Then they again called the man who was blind, and said to

him, Give God the praise: we know that this man is a sinner.
25 He answered and said, Whether he is a sinner or not, I do not know: one thing I know, that, whereas I was blind, now I see.
26 Then they said to him again, What did he do to you? how did he open your eyes?

9:25 Who is the Lord of the Ring? The man with an experience is not at the mercy of a man with an argument. This man *knew* that he was once blind and he *knew* that he could now see. No matter how others dispute it, that was his experience. The world may mock when someone is converted to Jesus Christ, but the Christian can say along with the writer of *Amazing Grace*, "I once was lost, but now am found; was blind, but now I see."

Many things happen when a sinner has the eyes of his understanding "enlightened" (Ephesians 2:18). Suddenly he becomes conscious of God. He has been like a fish in the ocean, looking for the ocean. Now he understands that God is omnipresent—that "in Him we live and move and have our being." However, this understanding dawned on him like the sun cracks the dawn. Before the Son of God fully shined in his heart, rays of light began to illuminate his understanding. His experience was like that of the prodigal son. Here's the story Jesus told of this wayward young man:

"A certain man had two sons: And the younger of them said to his father, Father, give me the portion of goods that falls to me. And he divided to them his livelihood. And not many days after, the younger son gathered all together, took his journey into a far country, and there wasted his substance with riotous living. And when he had spent all, there arose a mighty famine in that land; and he began to be in want. He went and joined himself to a citizen of that country; and he sent him into his fields to feed swine. And he would gladly have filled his belly with the husks that the swine ate: and no man gave him anything.

"But when he came to himself, he said, How many hired servants of my father's have bread enough and to spare, and I perish with hunger! I will arise and go to my father, and will say to him, Father, I have sinned against heaven and before you, and am no longer worthy to be called your son. Make me like one of your hired servants. And he arose and came to his father. But when he was yet a great way off, his father saw him and had compassion, and ran and fell on his neck and kissed him. And the son said to him, Father, I have sinned against heaven and in your sight, and am no longer worthy to be called your son. But the father said to his servants, Bring out the best robe and put it on him; and put a ring on his hand and shoes on his feet. And bring here the fatted calf and kill it; and let us eat and be merry: for this my son was dead and is alive again; he was lost and is found. And they began to be merry.

"Now his elder son was in the field: and as he came and drew near to the house, he heard music and dancing. So he called one of the servants and asked what these things meant. And he said to him, Your brother has come; and your father has killed the fatted calf, because he has received him safe and sound. And he was angry and would not go in: therefore his father came out and pleaded with him. And he answered and said to his father, Lo, these many years I have been serving you; I never transgressed your commandment at any time: and yet you never gave me a young goat, that I might make merry with my friends. But as soon as this your son came, who has devoured your livelihood with harlots, you have killed the fatted calf for him. And he said to him, Son, you are always with me, and all that I have is yours. It was right that we should make merry and be glad: for this your brother was dead and is alive again; and was lost and is found" (Luke 15:11–32).

Notice that the son's understanding come to him in adversity. This was well *before* he embraced his father. C. S. Lewis said that God whispers to us in our prosperity and shouts to us in our pain. Sometimes it takes adverse circumstances or a tragedy to stop us in our tracks and ask where God is. Also notice that it was when he realized that his appetites were for foul pig food that he came to his senses. Think about your future. Tragedy *will* strike. You *will* lose loved ones one day. Adversity crouches at the door. Ask the whereabouts of God now *before* it strikes.

Also, consider your appetites. Isn't it true that you love darkness more than light? Consider your heart's tastes in light of the fact that God considers lust to be the same as adultery (Matthew 5:27,28). Imagine if there had been a high-tech chip behind your ear that monitored your thought-life for the past six months, and the recording would be shown to your family. Wouldn't you feel ashamed? But that is what will happen on Judgment Day. God will bring to light every secret thing, whether it is good or evil, and those secret sins will come out as evidence of your guilt.

You have become a slave to unclean appetites. Let the rays of understanding that the Law of God brings cause you to come to your senses, get up out of the pigsty of your sinful condition before it's too late, and turn to the God who gave you life. He will meet you halfway and embrace you like a long lost son. He has already expressed His love for you on the cross. He will give you a robe of righteousness to cover your filth, and give you a ring for your finger . . . a ring that carries with it more than mere ornamentation.

The Old Testament speaks of rings giving the possessor the authority of life and death over others. It can be used for either good or evil. Genesis 41:42 informs us, "Pharaoh took off his ring from his hand, and put it upon Joseph's hand, and arrayed him in garments of fine linen, and put a gold chain around his neck." The ring gave Joseph *lordship* over Egypt. His word became law, and he used the authority it gave him to save many lives.

However, there was a man named Haman who used a ring for the furtherance of evil. The Bible tells us that this man was set in the kingdom "above all the princes" in Persia. All who saw him were obligated by the king's command to bow down and pay him homage. One man in the kingdom refused to bow his knee—a Jew named Mordecai. This infuriated Haman, so he sought to kill all the Jews throughout the land. He informed the king that there were people who did not keep the laws of his kingdom, and proposed that they be destroyed. We are then told, "The king took his ring from his hand and gave it to Haman, the son of Hammedatha the Agagite, the Jews' enemy." A decree was then made "to destroy, to kill, and to annihilate all the Jews, both young and old, little children and women, in one day"—the day before Passover. This was then sealed with the ring (see Esther 3:12). Because Haman possessed the ring, he had the authority to take the life of whomever he wanted. Haman became the lord of the ring.

When Mordecai still refused to pay homage, Haman had a gallows built on which to hang him. But through a series of strange circumstances, the king greatly honored Mordecai, and instead had Haman hung on his own gallows.

There is one whom the Bible calls "the prince of this world" (John 12:31) who, like Haman, had been given great authority. He had the power of death in his hand. In a sense, a ring was placed on the finger of this prince, and he had permission to devour the whole human race.

Satan is the name of this prince of darkness. He had authority over all who bow the knee to him through sin. The ring brings death to all who fall under sin's power. Like Haman, the god of this world had authority "to steal, and to kill, and to destroy" (John 10:10). He walks about like a roaring lion seeking whom he may devour (see 1 Peter 5:8).

There is only One human being who refused to bow down to Satan. He was also a Jew, and His name was Jesus of Nazareth. When they met, Satan offered Jesus the ultimate ring of power: "He showed him all the kingdoms of the world, and the glory of them; and said to him, All these things I will give you, if you will fall down and worship me." All Jesus had to do to possess the ring was to become a Satan worshiper. The devil tempted the Son of God, but He would not bow the knee. Temptation reveals the darker side of every one of us, but Jesus didn't have a "darker side." Sin had no power over the Lord of lords. He was sinless. This is what Jesus meant when He said, "The prince of this world comes and has nothing in me" (John 14:30).

The ring of sin had no influence over Jesus of Nazareth, so Satan had a "gallows" built for him—the cross. He proposed to hang Him from the cross until death, and to do so during the Passover. But the Bible says the dark lords of the underworld were ignorant that the cross was God's way of saving the human race from death. It was hidden from them: "Which none of the princes of this world knew: for had they known it, they would not have crucified the Lord of glory" (1 Corinthians 2:8). When Jesus rose from the dead, He stripped the devil of the power of death:

"...that through death he might destroy him who had the power of death, that is, the devil; and deliver them who through fear of death were all their lifetime subject to bondage" (Hebrews 2:14,15).

Notice the word "had." The prince no longer has his power. Satan was hung on his own gallows; the cross was his defeat. The human race may now be released from his icy grip.

If you allow the ring of sin to remain in your heart, it will deceive and destroy you. The Bible warns of the "deceitfulness of sin." Its seductive voice whispers of the pleasures of lust and power. Sin promises pleasure but brings with it unspeakable pain. Its golden sparkle has temporal delight but eternal consequences. Jesus said, "Whoever serves sin is a slave of sin." The door of delight is in truth the door of death. You cannot have sin without death (see Romans 6:23).

Are you still bowing to the prince of this world? Does the ring have power over you? Are you walking "according to the course of this world, according to the prince of the power of the air, the spirit who now works in the children of disobedience" (Ephesians 2:2)? Are you serving the enemy of your soul? Then cast the deceitful ring at the foot of the cross. Sin was dealt with at the cross of Calvary. If you won't take your sin to the cross, it will take you into the lake of fire (see Revelation 21:8).

In the story of the prodigal son, the ring was used for good. When the father put a ring on his son's finger, it meant more than "Welcome home, son." It meant that he was reinstated into the family.

Look now at how God the Father has given the ring of authority to His Son after His redemptive work on the cross: "Therefore God also has highly exalted him and given him a name which is above every name: that at the name of Jesus every knee should bow, of those in heaven, and those in earth, and those under the earth; and that every tongue should confess that Jesus Christ is Lord, to the glory of God the Father" (Philippians 2:9–11). *Everyone*—every ring-possessing lord, every demon, every single person ever born—will bow the knee to Jesus Christ, the King of kings and Lord of lords. The Bible says that the "mountains melt like wax at the presence of the LORD"; how much more then shall every golden ring of human authority melt into obscurity at the presence and power of His glory? You can either bow to Him in this life, acknowledge Him as Lord, and receive His great mercy—or you can stay in your sins and bow to Him in eternity and taste the bitterness of His justice. Yield your life to His Lordship today. There is no greater cause of celebration than when a sinner repents; it even makes heaven rejoice (see Luke 15:7).

Although God has given you life, He doesn't promise you tomorrow. The only thing you can be truly be sure of is the air going into your lungs at this moment. You cannot guarantee another breath; that comes by the grace of God—and you have greatly angered Him by your sin. Don't test His patience. All you have to decide is what to do with the life given you.

27 He answered them, I have told you already, and you did not hear: why would you hear it again? will you also be his disciples?

28 Then they reviled him, and said, You are his disciple; but we are Moses' disciples.

29 We know that God spoke to Moses: as for this fellow, we do not know where he is from.

30 The man answered and said to them, Why, this is a marvelous thing, that you do not know where he is from, and yet he has opened my eyes.

31 Now we know that God does not hear sinners: but if any man is a worshiper of God, and does his will, he hears him.

32 Since the world began it was unheard of that any man opened the eyes of one who was born blind.

33 If this man were not of God, he could do nothing.

34 They answered and said to him, You were altogether born in sins, and do you teach us? And they cast him out.

35 Jesus heard that they had cast him out; and when he had found him, he said to him, Do you believe on the Son of God?

36 He answered and said, Who is he, Lord, that I might believe on him?

37 And Jesus said to him, You have both seen him, and it is he who talks with you.

38 And he said, Lord, I believe. And he worshiped him.

39 And Jesus said, For judgment I have come into this world, that those who do not see might see; and that those who see might be made blind.

40 And some of the Pharisees who were with him heard these words, and said to him, Are we blind also?

41 Jesus said to them, If you were blind, you should have no sin: but now you say, We see; therefore your sin remains.

. . . .

9:33 It seems that this man had more than his physical eyes opened. He realized that this miracle was something only God could have done.

9:34 This statement reveals their proud self-righteousness.

9:38 Throughout Scripture where men worshiped other men or even angels, they were told to worship God only (see Revelation 19:10). Many times Jesus allowed people to worship Him. If He was not God, then He would have been transgressing God's Law by allowing worship of Himself.

CHAPTER 10

The Thief

VERILY, verily, I say to you, he who does not enter by the door into the sheepfold, but climbs up some other way, the same is a thief and a robber.

2 But he who enters in by the door is the shepherd of the sheep.

3 To him the doorkeeper opens; and the sheep hear his voice: and he calls his own sheep by name, and leads them out.

4 And when he puts forth his own sheep, he goes before them, and the sheep follow him: for they know his voice.

5 And a stranger they will not follow, but will flee from him: for they do not know the voice of strangers.

6 This parable Jesus spoke to them: but they did not understand the things which he spoke to them.

• •

10:2 In Psalm 23, David speaks of the Lord being his shepherd. Now the Shepherd Himself speaks.

10:6 The disciples continually lacked understanding of spiritual things until they were "born" of the Spirit on the Day of Pentecost. A Chinese toddler can understand and speak Chinese fluently, with far more expertise than the most intelligent of us who speak English. This is simply because he was born into the family and the Chinese language is his native tongue. Once we are born into the family of God, the things of God come naturally to us: "What man knows the things of a man except the spirit of man which is in him? even so no one knows the things of God except the Spirit of God. Now we have received, not the spirit of the world, but the Spirit who is of God; that we might know the things that are freely given to us of God. Which things also we speak, not in the words which man's wisdom teaches, but which the Holy Spirit teaches; comparing spiritual things with spiritual. But the natural man does not receive the things of the Spirit of God: for they are foolishness to him: neither can he know them, because they are spiritually discerned" (1 Corinthians 2:11–14).

7 Then Jesus said to them again, Verily, verily, I say to you, I am the door of the sheep.

8 All who ever came before me are thieves and robbers: but the sheep did not hear them.

9 I am the door: if any man enters in by me, he shall be saved, and shall go in and out and find pasture.

10 The thief does not come but to steal, and to kill, and to destroy: I have come that they might have life, and that they might have it more abundantly.

11 I am the good shepherd: the good shepherd gives his life for the sheep.

12 But he who is a hireling and not the shepherd, whose own the sheep are not, sees the wolf coming and leaves the sheep, and flees: and the wolf catches them, and scatters the sheep.

13 The hireling flees, because he is a hireling and does not care for the sheep.

14 I am the good shepherd, and know my sheep, and am known of mine.

15 As the Father knows me, even so I know the Father: and I lay down my life for the sheep.

16 And I have other sheep, which are not of this fold: them also I must bring, and they shall hear my voice; and there shall be one

· ·

10:10 The "thief" Jesus refers to is Satan, whom the Bible calls "the god of this world." He blinds the minds of those who do not trust in the Savior: "But if our gospel is veiled, it is veiled to those who are lost: In whom the god of this world has blinded the minds of those who do not believe, lest the light of the glorious gospel of Christ, who is the image of God, should shine to them" (2 Corinthians 4:3,4). The thief came to kill, steal, and destroy humans, who were made in the image of God. By contrast, Jesus Christ came that we may have life—spiritual life for all of eternity.

10:10 An abundant life doesn't mean "a happy life" as some maintain. It simply means "a full life."

10:12 The comparison of humanity to sheep is applicable—we scatter without a shepherd: "All we like sheep have gone astray; we have turned every one to his own way; and the Lord has laid on him the iniquity of us all" (Isaiah 53:6).

10:16 This is a reference to the fact that the gospel is for the Gentile as well as the Jew. The Bible says, "Is he the God of the Jews only? is he not also the God of the Gentiles? Yes, of the Gentiles also, since there is one God who will justify the circumcised by faith and the uncircumcised through faith" (Romans 3:29,30).

fold and one shepherd.

17 Therefore does my Father love me, because I lay down my life, that I might take it again.

18 No man takes it from me, but I lay it down of myself. I have power to lay it down, and I have power to take it again. This commandment I have received of my Father.

19 Therefore there was a division again among the Jews for these sayings.

20 And many of them said, He has a devil and is mad; why do you hear him?

21 Others said, These are not the words of him who has a devil. Can a devil open the eyes of the blind?

22 And it was the feast of the dedication at Jerusalem, and it was winter.

23 And Jesus walked in the temple in Solomon's porch.

24 Then the Jews surrounded him, and said to him, How long

• •

10:18   Jesus continually stated that He had come to earth to die. Here He reveals that men did not take His life from Him, nor did He *take* His own life through suicide. He freely *gave* Himself as a sacrifice for the sin of the world. Search the words of great men of history. See if you can find any who had the audacity to say that they had the power to resurrect themselves. If you do find one, see if you can find an empty tomb.

10:19   Whenever the gospel is preached, it *will* bring a division. The Word of God in the beginning brought a division between light and darkness (Genesis 1:4). So the same Word brings a division between light and darkness when it is preached in truth. It will divide husbands from wives, parents from their children, and children from their parents. Jesus likened its power to a sword. Look at His words:

> "Therefore whoever shall confess me before men, him I will also confess before my Father who is in heaven. But whoever shall deny me before men, him I will also deny before my Father who is in heaven. Do not think that I have come to send peace on earth: I did not come to send peace, but a sword. For I have come to set a man at variance against his father, and the daughter against her mother, and the daughter-in-law against her mother-in-law. And a man's foes shall be those of his own household. He who loves father or mother more than me is not worthy of me: and he who loves son or daughter more than me is not worthy of me. And he who does not take his cross and follow after me is not worthy of me. He who finds his life shall lose it: and he who loses his life for my sake shall find it" (Matthew 10:32–40).

do you keep us in doubt? If you are the Christ, tell us plainly.

25 Jesus answered them, I told you, and you did not believe: the works that I do in my Father's name, they bear witness of me.

26 But you do not believe, because you are not of my sheep, as I said to you.

27 My sheep hear my voice, and I know them, and they follow me:

28 And I give to them eternal life; and they shall never perish, neither shall any man pluck them out of my hand.

29 My Father, who gave them to me, is greater than all; and no man is able to pluck them out of my Father's hand.

30 I and my Father are one.

31 Then the Jews took up stones again to stone him.

32 Jesus answered them, Many good works I have shown you from my Father; for which of those works do you stone me?

33 The Jews answered him, saying, For a good work we do not stone you; but for blasphemy; and because you, being a man, make yourself God.

34 Jesus answered them, Is it not written in your law, I said, You are gods?

35 If he called them gods, to whom the word of God came, and the scripture cannot be broken;

36 Do you say of him, whom the Father has sanctified and sent into the world, You blaspheme; because I said, I am the Son of

• •

10:21 The dichotomy is that either Jesus was mad or He was God. If He was insane, then close this book and forget Him. However, you have the same dilemma as those who heard Him and saw His supernatural works. Can a mad man open the eyes of the blind? Our most brilliant doctors don't know how to open the eyes of one born blind. Does a mad man have gracious words pour from His lips? We are therefore left with the conclusion that this Man *must* be from God as He claimed, and His words must be true. The eternal implications are sobering.

10:25 In this discourse (verses 25–30), Jesus calls God His Father three times and then climaxes with the incredible statement that He and the Father are one. How can the two be one? It has been rightly said that when God, the upholder of the universe, became a Man, He didn't cease to be the upholder of the universe. He created for Himself a human body and then filled that body as a hand fills a glove. The Bible calls Jesus "the image of the invisible God" (Colossians 1:15). Jesus' words caused the Jews to pick up stones to execute Him for blasphemy (verses 31–39).

God?

37 If I do not do the works of my Father, do not believe me.

38 But if I do, though you do not believe me, believe the works: that you may know and believe that the Father is in me, and I in him.

39 Therefore they sought again to take him: but he escaped out of their hand,

40 And went away again beyond Jordan into the place where John at first baptized; and there he remained.

41 And many came to him, and said, John did no miracle: but all things that John spoke of this man were true.

42 And many believed on him there.

CHAPTER 11

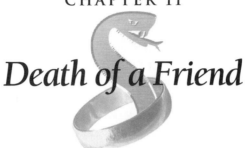

Death of a Friend

NOW a certain man was sick, named Lazarus of Bethany, the town of Mary and her sister Martha.

2 (It was that Mary who anointed the Lord with ointment, and wiped his feet with her hair, whose brother Lazarus was sick.)

3 Therefore his sisters sent to him, saying, Lord, behold, he whom you love is sick.

4 When Jesus heard that, he said, This sickness is not to death, but for the glory of God, that the Son of God might be glorified thereby.

5 Now Jesus loved Martha, and her sister, and Lazarus.

6 When he had heard therefore that he was sick, he remained two days in the same place where he was.

7 Then after that he said to his disciples, Let us go into Judea again.

8 His disciples said to him, Master, lately the Jews sought to stone you; and you go there again?

9 Jesus answered, Are there not twelve hours in the day? If any man walks in the day, he does not stumble, because he sees the

. . . .

11:6 This verse gives us some insight into the mystery of why God doesn't always *immediately* answer prayer. The Bible makes it clear that Jesus loved Lazarus (verses 3, 36), and yet when He heard that Lazarus was sick, He stayed where He was for two days, allowing Lazarus to die. Sometimes God will delay answering prayer so that He might work out His great purposes in our lives (see verses 15, 42).  Other times God will completely disregard our prayer because of sin in our lives (see Psalm 66:18 and Isaiah 59:1,2).

light of this world.

10 But if a man walks in the night, he stumbles, because there is no light in him.

11 These things he said: and after that he said to them, Our friend Lazarus sleeps; but I go, that I may awake him out of sleep.

12 Then his disciples said, Lord, if he sleeps, he shall do well.

13 However, Jesus spoke of his death: but they thought that he had spoken of taking rest in sleep.

14 Then Jesus said to them plainly, Lazarus is dead.

15 And I am glad for your sakes that I was not there, to the intent you may believe; nevertheless let us go to him.

16 Then said Thomas, who is called Didymus, to his fellow disciples, Let us also go, that we may die with him.

17 Then when Jesus came, he found that he had lain in the grave four days already.

18 Now Bethany was near Jerusalem, about fifteen furlongs off:

19 And many of the Jews came to Martha and Mary, to comfort them concerning their brother.

20 Then Martha, as soon as she heard that Jesus was coming, went and met him: but Mary still sat in the house.

21 Then Martha said to Jesus, Lord, if you had been here, my brother would not have died.

22 But even now I know that whatever you will ask of God, God will give it to you.

23 Jesus said to her, Your brother shall rise again.

24 Martha said to him, I know that he shall rise again in the resurrection at the last day.

25 Jesus said to her, I am the resurrection and the life: he who believes in me, though he were dead, yet shall he live:

26 And whoever lives and believes in me shall never die. Do you believe this?

• •

11:18 The modern equivalent is two miles.

11:26 Do *you* believe this? If you believe something, your belief will direct your actions. If you believe that there are landmines in front of you, you will govern your steps by your belief. If you believe that Jesus is the resurrection and the life, then you will repent and trust in Him as Lord and Savior. Have you done that? If not, why not? God doesn't want you to go to hell. You don't want to go to hell. I don't want you to go to hell. Death could seize upon you before you finish reading this sentence. We are talking about your eternity.

27 She said to him, Yes, Lord: I believe that you are the Christ, the Son of God, who should come into the world.

28 And when she had said this, she went her way, and called Mary her sister secretly, saying, The Master has come, and calls for you.

29 As soon as she heard that, she arose quickly and came to him.

30 Now Jesus had not yet come into the town, but was in that place where Martha met him.

. . . .

Please, don't put it off any longer. Humble yourself, repent by confessing and turning from your sins, then trust Jesus with your eternal salvation.

There are many who believe that Jesus is the Christ, that He is God in human form, that He died on the cross, etc., *but they don't obey Him.* Look at the fearful fate of these people: "...the Lord Jesus shall be revealed from heaven with his mighty angels, in flaming fire taking vengeance on those who do not know God, and who do not obey the gospel of our Lord Jesus Christ: who shall be punished with everlasting destruction from the presence of the Lord, and from the glory of his power" (2 Thessalonians 1:7–9). Consider to whom these words are addressed: "Not everyone who says to me, Lord, Lord, shall enter into the kingdom of heaven; but he who does the will of my Father in heaven. Many will say to me in that day, Lord, Lord, have we not prophesied in your name? and in your name cast out devils? and in your name done many wonderful works? And then I will profess to them, I never knew you: depart from me, you who work iniquity. Therefore whoever hears these sayings of mine, and does them, I will liken him to a wise man who built his house upon a rock: And the rain descended, and the floods came, and the winds blew and beat upon that house; and it did not fall: for it was founded upon a rock. And everyone who hears these sayings of mine, and does not do them, shall be likened to a foolish man who built his house upon the sand: And the rain descended, and the floods came, and the winds blew and beat upon that house; and it fell: and great was the fall of it" (Matthew 7:21–27).

You are not promised tomorrow. When tragedy strikes, it is human nature to say, "I never thought it would happen to me." However, every day 150,000 people (who no doubt have the same love of life that you have) are swallowed by death, and you can be certain that almost all of them said, "I never thought it would happen to me." As sure as hell, death will come to each of us, so today strip death of its power by calling on the One who is the resurrection and the life. Don't listen to the whisperings of demons any longer—call out to Him who said, "I am he who lives, and was dead; and, behold, I am alive forevermore, amen; and I have the keys of hell and of Death" (Revelation 1:18). (The demonic realm is very real. See www.raycomfort.com/exorcism.)

31 Then the Jews who were with her in the house and comforted her, when they saw that Mary rose up hastily and went out, followed her, saying, She goes to the grave to weep there.

32 Then when Mary came where Jesus was, and saw him, she fell down at his feet, saying to him, Lord, if you had been here, my brother would not have died.

33 When Jesus therefore saw her weeping, and the Jews also weeping who came with her, he groaned in the spirit, and was troubled,

34 And said, Where have you laid him? They said to him, Lord, come and see.

35 Jesus wept.

36 Then said the Jews, Behold how he loved him!

37 And some of them said, Could not this man, who opened the eyes of the blind, have caused that even this man should not have died?

38 Jesus therefore again groaning in himself came to the grave. It was a cave, and a stone lay upon it.

39 Jesus said, Take away the stone. Martha, the sister of him who was dead, said to him, Lord, by this time he stinks: for he has been dead four days.

40 Jesus said to her, Did I not say to you that, if you would believe, you should see the glory of God?

41 Then they took away the stone from the place where the dead was laid. And Jesus lifted up his eyes, and said, Father, I thank you that you have heard me.

42 And I know that you always hear me: but because of the people who stand by I said it, that they may believe that you have sent me.

43 And when he had thus spoken, he cried with a loud voice, Lazarus, come forth.

44 And he who was dead came forth, bound hand and foot with graveclothes: and his face was bound about with a cloth. Jesus said to them, Loose him, and let him go.

45 Then many of the Jews who came to Mary, and had seen the things which Jesus did, believed on him.

· ·

11:43 It has been well said that if Jesus had not called Lazarus by name, the whole graveyard would have been emptied.

46 But some of them went away to the Pharisees, and told them what things Jesus had done.

47 Then the chief priests and the Pharisees gathered a council, and said, What shall we do? for this man does many miracles.

48 If we let him thus alone, all men will believe on him: and the Romans shall come and take away both our place and nation.

49 And one of them, named Caiaphas, being the high priest that same year, said to them, You know nothing at all,

50 Nor consider that it is expedient for us, that one man should die for the people, and that the whole nation not perish.

51 And this he spoke not of himself: but being high priest that year, he prophesied that Jesus should die for that nation;

52 And not for that nation only, but also that he should gather together in one the children of God who were scattered abroad.

53 Then from that day forth they took counsel together to put him to death.

54 Therefore Jesus no longer walked openly among the Jews; but went to a country near the wilderness, into a city called Ephraim, and there continued with his disciples.

55 And the Jews' Passover was near at hand: and many went out of the country up to Jerusalem before the Passover, to purify themselves.

56 Then they sought for Jesus, and spoke among themselves as they stood in the temple, What do you think, that he will not come to the feast?

57 Now both the chief priests and the Pharisees had given a commandment, that if any man knew where he was, he should show it, that they might take him.

• •

11:46 It is believed by most that diamond is the hardest substance in creation. Not so. It is the human heart. These men witnessed the miracle of the resurrection of a four-day-dead stinking corpse, and yet they still hardened their heart. Perhaps you have been guilty of doing the same thing. Maybe you have lived your life surrounded by the miracle of creation, and haven't given God a moment's serious thought. Listen to the birds, look at the flowers, gaze in wonder at a sunrise, think of the marvels of the human eye, let your ear drink in the sounds of a babbling brook, then ponder the power of the One who created these things. Open your heart to Him. Martin Luther said that if the greatest commandment is to love God with heart, mind, soul, and strength, then the greatest sin is failure to do so.

CHAPTER 12

The Living Dead

THEN six days before the Passover Jesus came to Bethany, where Lazarus was who had been dead, whom he raised from the dead.

2 There they made him a supper; and Martha served: but Lazarus was one of those who sat at the table with him.

3 Then Mary took a pound of ointment of spikenard, very costly, and anointed the feet of Jesus, and wiped his feet with her hair: and the house was filled with the odor of the ointment.

4 Then one of his disciples, Judas Iscariot, Simon's son, who should betray him, said,

5 Why was this ointment not sold for three hundred pence, and given to the poor?

6 He said this, not that he cared for the poor; but because he was a thief, and had the bag, and took what was put in it.

7 Then Jesus said, Let her alone: she has kept this for the day of my burying.

8 For the poor you always have with you; but me you will not have always.

9 Many of the Jews therefore knew that he was there: and they came not for Jesus' sake only, but that they might see Lazarus also, whom he had raised from the dead.

10 But the chief priests consulted that they might also put Lazarus to death;

11 Because by reason of him many of the Jews went away, and

. . . .

12:5   This amount was the annual wage of a working man.

12:6   Judas Iscariot was a hypocrite. He was a thief who had been trusted as the treasurer, and yet he was stealing from the money bag.

believed on Jesus.

12 On the next day many people who had come to the feast, when they heard that Jesus was coming to Jerusalem,

13 Took branches of palm trees, and went forth to meet him, and cried, Hosanna: Blessed is the King of Israel who comes in the name of the Lord.

14 And Jesus, when he had found a young donkey, sat on it; as it is written,

15 Fear not, daughter of Zion: behold, your King comes, sitting on a donkey's colt.

16 These things his disciples did not understand at first: but when Jesus was glorified, then they remembered that these things were written of him, and that they had done these things to him.

17 Therefore the people who were with him when he called Lazarus out of his grave, and raised him from the dead, bore record.

18 For this cause the people also met him, for they heard that he had done this miracle.

19 The Pharisees therefore said among themselves, Do you perceive how you accomplish nothing? behold, the world has gone after him.

• •

12:10 Christians shouldn't marvel when the world hates them. Jesus warned that the world may even kill His followers, thinking that they were doing God a favor. See John 16:2.

12:14 God takes the foolish things of this world to confound the wise. He chooses to be born in a stable, not a palace, and to ride on a donkey, not on a stallion. Even the message of salvation uses this principle: "For the preaching of the cross is foolishness to those who are perishing; but to us who are saved it is the power of God. For it is written, I will destroy the wisdom of the wise, and will bring to nothing the understanding of the prudent. Where is the wise? where is the scribe? where is the disputer of this world? Has not God made foolish the wisdom of this world?...For you see your calling, brethren, that not many wise men according to the flesh, not many mighty, not many noble, are called. But God has chosen the foolish things of the world to confound the wise; and God has chosen the weak things of the world to confound the things which are mighty; and base things of the world, and things which are despised, God has chosen, yes, and things which are not, to bring to nothing things that are: that no flesh should glory in his presence" (1 Corinthians 1:18–20,26–29).

12:15 This is a fulfillment of a prophecy recorded in Zechariah 9:9.

20 And there were certain Greeks among them who came up to worship at the feast:

21 The same came therefore to Philip, who was of Bethsaida of Galilee, and desired him, saying, Sir, we would see Jesus.

22 Philip came and told Andrew: and again Andrew and Philip told Jesus.

23 And Jesus answered them, saying, The hour has come that the Son of man should be glorified.

24 Verily, verily, I say to you, Except a grain of wheat falls into the ground and dies, it abides alone: but if it dies, it brings forth much fruit.

25 He who loves his life shall lose it; and he who hates his life in this world shall keep it to eternal life.

26 If any man serves me, let him follow me; and where I am, there also shall my servant be: if any man serves me, him will my Father honor.

27 Now my soul is troubled; and what shall I say? Father, save me from this hour: but for this cause I came to this hour.

• •

12:25 Do you love your life? If you seek to keep it, you will lose it. You are in a battle with Almighty God (remember that the Bible says you are an enemy of God in your mind through wicked works—Colossians 1:21). Don't fight against Him. You have more chance of fighting off lightning with a feather duster. Eternal justice calls for your blood. You have sinned against God, and you must therefore die. Your only hope is to be made right with your Creator. Give up. Surrender. Admit defeat. Lay down your arms. Cry out, "God be merciful to me, a sinner." He is rich in mercy to *all* who call upon Him.

Religion can't save you. It can't change the heart. Those who rely on religion to save them are like a vicious serial killer who has slit the throats of innocent women, thinking that he will be acquitted in the courtroom if he wears a clean pressed suit. No amount of religious deeds or good works will bribe the Judge to pervert eternal justice. Our crimes cry out for justice no matter what we do to try to cleanse ourselves in His sight.

How then can a sinful man be made righteous before a holy God? Scripture has the answer: "If you shall confess with your mouth the Lord Jesus, and shall believe in your heart that God has raised him from the dead, you shall be saved. For with the heart man believes to righteousness; and with the mouth confession is made to salvation. For the scripture says, Whoever believes on him shall not be ashamed. For there is no difference between the Jew and the Greek: for the same Lord over all is rich to all who call upon him. For whoever shall call upon the name of the Lord shall be saved" (Romans 10:9–13).

28 Father, glorify your name. Then there came a voice from heaven, saying, I have both glorified it, and will glorify it again.

29 Therefore the people who stood by and heard it said that it thundered: others said, An angel spoke to him.

30 Jesus answered and said, This voice came not because of me, but for your sakes.

31 Now is the judgment of this world: now shall the prince of this world be cast out.

32 And I, if I be lifted up from the earth, will draw all men to me.

33 This he said, signifying what death he should die.

34 The people answered him, We have heard out of the law that Christ abides forever: and how do you say, The Son of man must be lifted up? who is this Son of man?

35 Then Jesus said to them, Yet a little while is the light with you. Walk while you have the light, lest darkness come upon you: for he who walks in darkness does not know where he goes.

36 While you have light, believe in the light, that you may be the children of light. These things Jesus spoke, and departed, and hid himself from them.

37 But though he had done so many miracles before them, yet they did not believe on him:

38 That the saying of Isaiah the prophet might be fulfilled, which he spoke, Lord, who has believed our report? and to whom has the arm of the Lord been revealed?

39 Therefore they could not believe, because Isaiah said again,

40 He has blinded their eyes, and hardened their heart; that they should not see with their eyes, nor understand with their heart, and be converted, and I should heal them.

41 These things Isaiah said, when he saw his glory, and spoke of him.

42 Nevertheless among the chief rulers also many believed on him; but because of the Pharisees they did not confess him, lest they should be put out of the synagogue:

. . . .

12:27 Again Jesus speaks of the reason for His coming to earth. He came to suffer and die for the sins of the world.

12:32 He knew from the beginning that He would be crucified. See John 3:14.

12:38 This is a fulfillment of a prophecy recorded in Isaiah 53:1.

43 For they loved the praise of men more than the praise of God.

44 Jesus cried and said, He who believes on me, does not believe on me, but on him who sent me.

45 And he who sees me sees him who sent me.

46 I have come as a light into the world, that whoever believes on me should not abide in darkness.

47 And if any man hears my words, and does not believe, I do not judge him: for I did not come to judge the world, but to save the world.

48 He who rejects me, and does not receive my words, has one who judges him: the word that I have spoken, the same shall judge him in the last day.

49 For I have not spoken of myself; but the Father who sent me, he gave me a commandment, what I should say, and what I should speak.

50 And I know that his commandment is life everlasting: therefore whatever I speak, even as the Father said to me, so I speak.

. . . .

12:43   What is stopping you from trusting in the Savior today? Is it the praise of men? Praises quickly fade. Applause is but for a moment. It can fill the ears but leave the heart empty. The same people who compliment you to your face will often gossip about you behind your back. The smile of God is infinitely more important that the smile of the world. You cannot have both.

12:44   Again Jesus establishes that whoever has seen Him has seen God. He who believes on Him (trusts in Him) believes on God. Jesus is the light of the world, and all who trust in Him will not abide in darkness. Think of how the world lives in darkness. People don't know where they came from. They don't know the future. They have no idea what causes death or what will happen to them after they die. They sit in the dark shadow of death, waiting for it to come to them. The tragedy is that they are willfully ignorant. They *will* not come to Him that they might have life (John 5:40).

12:47   This is a reiteration of John 3:17. However, the time will come when the Word of God will judge the world (verse 48).

12:50   God commands you to obey Him *that you might live.*

CHAPTER 13

Who Is It?

NOW before the feast of the Passover, when Jesus knew that his hour had come that he should depart out of this world to the Father, having loved his own who were in the world, he loved them to the end.

2 And supper being ended, the devil having now put into the heart of Judas Iscariot, Simon's son, to betray him;

3 Jesus knowing that the Father had given all things into his hands, and that he had come from God, and went to God;

4 He rose from supper and laid aside his garments; and took a towel and girded himself.

5 After that he poured water into a basin, and began to wash the disciples' feet, and to wipe them with the towel with which he was girded.

6 Then he came to Simon Peter: and Peter said to him, Lord, do you wash my feet?

7 Jesus answered and said to him, What I do you do not know now; but you shall know after this.

8 Peter said to him, You shall never wash my feet. Jesus answered him, If I do not wash you, you have no part with me.

9 Simon Peter said to him, Lord, not my feet only, but also my hands and my head.

· ·

13:1   Once again there is mention of the "hour" for which Jesus was born.

13:2   Although we are all responsible for our own sinful actions, the Bible tells us that there is a spiritual battle surrounding us (see Ephesians 6:12). Again, there is a "spirit" that "works in the children of disobedience." If we realized where thoughts of homosexuality, sexual perversions, murder, rape, etc., originate, we may be less likely to embrace them.

10 Jesus said to him, He who is washed needs only to wash his feet, but is completely clean: and you are clean, but not all.

11 For he knew who should betray him; therefore he said, You are not all clean.

12 So after he had washed their feet, and had taken his garments, and sat down again, he said to them, Do you know what I have done to you?

13 You call me Master and Lord: and you say well; for so I am.

14 If I then, your Lord and Master, have washed your feet; you also ought to wash one another's feet.

15 For I have given you an example, that you should do as I have done to you.

16 Verily, verily, I say to you, The servant is not greater than his lord; neither is he who is sent greater than he who sent him.

17 If you know these things, happy are you if you do them.

18 I do not speak of you all: I know whom I have chosen: but that the scripture may be fulfilled, He who eats bread with me has lifted up his heel against me.

19 Now I tell you before it comes, that, when it does come to pass, you may believe that I am he.

20 Verily, verily, I say to you, He who receives whomever I send receives me; and he who receives me receives him who sent me.

21 When Jesus had thus said, he was troubled in spirit, and testified and said, Verily, verily, I say to you, that one of you shall betray me.

22 Then the disciples looked on one another, doubting of whom he spoke.

23 Now there was leaning on Jesus' bosom one of his disciples, whom Jesus loved.

24 Simon Peter therefore beckoned to him, that he should ask who it should be of whom he spoke.

· ·

13:17 This is the only mention in the New Testament of "happiness." If you want to find it in this life, become a servant of humanity . . . and the greatest way you can serve them is to lead them to the Savior.

13:18 This is a fulfillment of a prophecy recorded in Psalm 41:9.

13:22 Judas was such a deceiver that he had even fooled the other disciples. He had pretended to be a follower of Jesus for three years, and rather than suspect the trustworthy treasurer, they suspected each other. Hypocrites may fool humanity, but they *cannot* fool God. See John 13:35 comment.

25 He then lying on Jesus' breast said to him, Lord, who is it?

26 Jesus answered, It is he to whom I shall give a piece of bread, when I have dipped it. And when he had dipped the bread, he gave it to Judas Iscariot, the son of Simon.

27 And after the piece of bread Satan entered into him. Then Jesus said to him, What you do, do quickly.

28 Now no man at the table knew for what intent he spoke this to him.

29 For some of them thought, because Judas had the bag, that Jesus had said to him, Buy those things that we have need of for the feast; or, that he should give something to the poor.

30 Then, having received the piece of bread, he went immediately out: and it was night.

31 Therefore, when he had gone out, Jesus said, Now is the Son of man glorified, and God is glorified in him.

32 If God be glorified in him, God shall also glorify him in himself, and shall immediately glorify him.

33 Little children, yet a little while I am with you. You shall seek me: and as I said to the Jews, Where I go, you cannot come; so

. . . .

13:30 Years ago, California police conducted a sting operation. They had a list of thousands of wanted criminals who had somehow evaded jail. Rather than risking their lives by attempting to arrest each one, they sent all the criminals a letter telling them they had won a large amount of money in a drawing. The police put signs and banners on a building, and placed balloons and even a clown on the outside to create a festive atmosphere in order to welcome the "winners." As each criminal entered the building, he heard music and other sounds of celebration. He was then ushered into a room where he smiled as his hand was shaken. The facial expression changed from joy to unbelief as each was told, "Congratulations, you have just won time in prison!" Dozens of criminals made their way through the main doors, were arrested and ushered out the back door.

It was interesting to note that many of the lawbreakers admitted, "I *thought* it was a sting operation!" but their greed wouldn't let them stay away. Their love of money blinded them to reason. Judas was also blinded by his love of money. Think deeply about the issue of *eternity*, asking yourself, "What shall it profit a man if he shall gain the whole world, and lose his own soul?" (Mark 8:36).

now I say to you.

34 A new commandment I give to you, That you love one another; as I have loved you, that you also love one another.

35 By this shall all men know that you are my disciples, if you have love for one another.

36 Simon Peter said to him, Lord, where are you going? Jesus answered him, Where I go, you cannot follow me now; but you shall follow me afterwards.

37 Peter said to him, Lord, why cannot I follow you now? I will lay down my life for your sake.

38 Jesus answered him, Will you lay down your life for my sake? Verily, verily, I say to you, The cock shall not crow, till you have denied me three times.

· ·

13:35 The evidence that someone is genuinely converted and truly a disciple of Jesus is a love for other Christians. One of the greatest hindrances to people coming to Christ is blatant hypocrisy within Christianity. Many complain, "The church is full of hypocrites, and besides, nothing has caused more wars in history than religion." No argument there. But let's look at what a hypocrite is. The word means "pretender." In other words, the hypocrite is a non-Christian who is pretending to be a Christian. He's not on our side, he's on yours.

The way bank employees are trained to recognize counterfeit bills is to study the genuine article. When they see the false, they can identify it because their eye is trained to know the real thing. The real thing in Christianity is someone who is faithful, kind, loving, good, gentle, humble, patient, self-controlled, and will speak the truth in love. So the next time you're watching TV and see a black-hatted, booze-sodden, Old-English speaking, Bible-quoting hypocrite plunge a pitchfork into his neighbor's back "in the name of the Lord," ask yourself, "Is this a genuine Christian? Does he love his neighbor as himself? Is he kind, gentle, and good, generous, self-controlled? Does he love his enemies? Does he do good to those who spitefully use him?" If not, then you have another non-Christian who is pretending to be a Christian. Hypocrites may sit *within* the Church, but they are not part *of* the Church. The true Church is made up of genuine believers. God knows those who love Him and He will sort out the true and the false on the Day of Judgment.

13:37 Peter had the words but not the heart to truly follow Jesus. It would take a new heart (a new birth) to create the man God wanted him to be. This happened on the Day of Pentecost (see Acts chapters 1 and 2). Some people are concerned that if they become Christians, they won't be able to live for God or to resist the sin they so love. That is the miracle of the new birth. God Himself gives us a new heart that longs to please Him, and He also gives us the power of His Holy Spirit to help us in our weaknesses so we will do what we know we should.

CHAPTER 14

Do Not Be Afraid

DO NOT let your heart be troubled: you believe in God, believe also in me.

2 In my Father's house are many mansions: if it were not so, I would have told you. I go to prepare a place for you.

3 And if I go and prepare a place for you, I will come again and receive you to myself; that where I am, there you may be also.

4 And where I go you know, and the way you know.

5 Thomas said to him, Lord, we do not know where you go; and how can we know the way?

6 Jesus said to him, I am the way, the truth, and the life: no man comes to the Father, but by me.

. . . .

14:6 In one sweeping statement, Jesus brushes aside every manmade religion and says that they cannot bring any man or woman to God. This is intolerant, exclusive, offensive—but true. A holy God will not *tolerate* sin of any sort. His plan of salvation is *exclusive* to those who obey Him, and this is utterly *offensive* to self-righteous humanity, who insist that they can purchase immortality by their own religious works. The Bible tells us why they are deceived into thinking this: "For they being ignorant of God's righteousness, and going about to establish their own righteousness, have not submitted themselves to the righteousness of God" (Romans 10:3). If religious people understood that on the Day of Judgment they will have to face a perfect Law (Psalm 19:7), and that God is perfect and therefore demands perfection in thought, word, and deed (Matthew 5:48), then they might not be so quick to think that *they* can make peace with Him themselves.

Imagine that you are a criminal, standing in the courtroom guilty of a very serious crime. There is a $500,000 fine to pay. You don't have two cents to rub together, but you tell the judge that you cleaned his car on the way to court. Will the judge therefore let you go? Of course not. The only grounds on which he may dismiss your case is if someone pays your fine. That's what God did for

7 If you had known me, you should have known my Father also: and from now on you know him, and have seen him.

8 Philip said to him, Lord, show us the Father, and it is sufficient for us.

9 Jesus said to him, Have I been so long with you, and yet you have not known me, Philip? he who has seen me has seen the Father; and how do you say then, Show us the Father?

10 Do you not believe that I am in the Father, and the Father in me? the words that I speak to you I do not speak of myself: but the Father who dwells in me, he does the works.

11 Believe me that I am in the Father, and the Father in me: or else believe me for the very works' sake.

12 Verily, verily, I say to you, He who believes on me, the works that I do he shall do also; and greater works than these shall he do; because I go to my Father.

13 And whatever you shall ask in my name, that I will do, that the Father may be glorified in the Son.

14 If you shall ask anything in my name, I will do it.

15 If you love me, keep my commandments.

16 And I will pray the Father, and he shall give you another

· ·

us through the cross.

It is interesting to note that when Christians proclaim this biblical truth, they are accused of being "intolerant." It seems that those who accuse others of intolerance are themselves tolerant of everything *but* Christianity. They cannot tolerate the Bible's claim that the way of salvation is exclusive to Jesus Christ. However, for a Christian to say that there is any other way to God is to bear false witness. The Bible makes it clear that there is no other way to salvation than through Jesus Christ: "Neither is there salvation in any other: for there is no other name under heaven given among men, by which we must be saved" (Acts 4:12), "Whoever transgresses and does not abide in the doctrine of Christ, does not have God. He who abides in the doctrine of Christ has both the Father and the Son" (2 John 9).

Notice also that Jesus said the only way a person "comes to the Father" is by "Me." Salvation is not modeling your lifestyle after a person. Salvation comes through having *the* person of Jesus Christ as your Lord and Savior.

14:9   Again, Jesus says that He is God manifest in human form. This is the teaching of the Bible: "And without controversy great is the mystery of godliness: God was manifested in the flesh, justified in the Spirit, seen of angels, preached unto the Gentiles, believed on in the world, received up into glory" (1 Timothy 3:16).

Comforter, that he may abide with you forever;

17 Even the Spirit of truth; whom the world cannot receive, because it does not see him, nor know him: but you know him; for he dwells with you, and shall be in you.

18 I will not leave you comfortless: I will come to you.

19 Yet a little while, and the world sees me no more; but you see me: because I live, you shall live also.

20 At that day you shall know that I am in my Father, and you in me, and I in you.

21 He who has my commandments and keeps them, it is he who loves me: and he who loves me shall be loved of my Father, and I will love him, and will manifest myself to him.

· ·

14:14 Some look at this open-ended promise and assume that they can ask for a new Mercedes; then when God doesn't come through, they think it proves that this promise (and others) are empty. However, the rule of biblical interpretation is to interpret Scripture with Scripture. God will not give something to His children unless it is within His permissive will: "This is the confidence that we have in him, that if we ask anything *according to his will*, he hears us. And if we know that he hears us, whatever we ask, we know that we have the petitions that we desired of him" (1 John 5:14,15, emphasis added).

14:15 The only real evidence that someone loves God is a heart obedient to His will.

14:17 Jesus is speaking of the fact that the Christian has the Holy Spirit living within him. This is a fulfillment of an Old Testament promise: "I will give you a new heart, and I will put a new spirit within you: and I will take away the stony heart out of your flesh, and I will give you a heart of flesh. And I will put my Spirit within you and cause you to walk in my statutes, and you shall keep my judgments and do them" (Ezekiel 36:26,27). God "seals" the believer with the Holy Spirit: "In him you also trusted, after you heard the word of truth, the gospel of your salvation: in whom also, after you believed, you were sealed with that Holy Spirit of promise" (Ephesians 1:13).

14:19 The resurrection of Jesus Christ meant that the door of eternal salvation would open to all who trust in Him.

14:21 Read that promise again. Either it is true or it isn't. The proof of the pudding is in the tasting. The Bible tells us to "taste and see that the LORD is good" (Psalm 34:8). Your bluff is being called. Stop analyzing the pudding; taste it. If you obey the words of Jesus, He will reveal Himself to you.

Imagine that you tried to describe a television to someone who had never seen one. You explain, "When you press this button, a person comes on and reads the up-to-date news to you—often as it happens." Your skeptical friend asks,

22 Judas, not Iscariot, said to him, Lord, how is it that you will manifest yourself to us, and not to the world?

23 Jesus answered and said to him, If a man loves me, he will keep my words: and my Father will love him, and we will come to him and make our home with him.

24 He who does not love me does not keep my sayings: and the word which you hear is not mine, but the Father's who sent me.

25 These things I have spoken to you, being yet present with you.

26 But the Comforter, who is the Holy Spirit, whom the Father will send in my name, he shall teach you all things, and bring all things to your remembrance, whatever I have said to you.

27 Peace I leave with you, my peace I give to you: not as the world gives, do I give to you. Do not let your heart be troubled, nor let it be afraid.

28 You have heard how I said to you, I go away and come again to you. If you loved me, you would rejoice, because I said, I go to the Father: for my Father is greater than I.

• •

"How does he get into the box?" You reply, "He's not actually in the box." He says, "Is he in there or isn't he?" You answer, "Well, his image is sent via invisible television signals through the air to an antenna, down a wire, up a cord, and into the box." Your friend becomes a little impatient and says, "So this newsreader of yours flies invisibly through the air, slides down an antenna, crawls up a cord, and into your set. What sort of simpleton do you think I am?"

Your confidence isn't shaken because you can prove your claim, fantastic though it may sound. You pass him the remote-control and say, "Push the button and see for yourself."

True, the claim of the Christian faith is fantastic in the truest sense of the word —repent and trust in Jesus Christ, and the invisible God of creation will reveal Himself to you (John 14:21). Our confidence isn't shaken in the face of a skeptical world, simply because the claim *can* be proven. Skeptic, push the button of repentance toward God and faith toward the Lord Jesus Christ, and you will experience the miracle of conversion.

14:28 This is a favorite verse of Jehovah's Witnesses to try to prove that Jesus was a mere creation of Jehovah—a lesser god. They are forgetting that the rule of biblical interpretation is to compare Scripture with Scripture. The reason Jesus said that the Father was greater was because at that point of time it was true. In His incarnation (becoming human), even the angels were greater than Him: "But we see Jesus, who was made a little lower than the angels for the suffering of death, crowned with glory and honor; that he by the grace of God should taste death for every man" (Hebrews 2:9).

29 And now I have told you before it came to pass, that, when it does come to pass, you might believe.

30 Hereafter I will not talk much with you: for the prince of this world comes, and has nothing in me.

31 But that the world may know that I love the Father; and as the Father gave me commandment, even so I do. Arise, let us go from here.

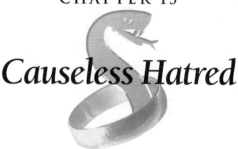

CHAPTER 15

Causeless Hatred

I AM the true vine, and my Father is the vinedresser.

2 Every branch in me that does not bear fruit he takes away: and every branch that bears fruit, he purges it, that it may bring forth more fruit.

3 Now you are clean through the word which I have spoken to you.

4 Abide in me, and I in you. As the branch cannot bear fruit of itself, except it abides in the vine; no more can you, except you abide in me.

5 I am the vine, you are the branches: He who abides in me, and I in him, the same brings forth much fruit: for without me you can do nothing.

6 If a man does not abide in me, he is cast forth as a branch, and is withered; and men gather them, and cast them into the fire, and they are burned.

7 If you abide in me, and my words abide in you, you shall ask what you will, and it shall be done to you.

8 Herein is my Father glorified, that you bear much fruit; so shall you be my disciples.

9 As the Father has loved me, so I have loved you: continue in my love.

10 If you keep my commandments, you shall abide in my love;

. . . .

15:5 Certain "fruits" should be evident in the lives of those who are in Christ: the fruit of repentance, holiness, praise, thanksgiving, and the fruit of the Spirit—love, joy, peace, longsuffering, gentleness, goodness, faith, meekness, and self-control (Galatians 5:22).

even as I have kept my Father's commandments, and abide in his love.

11 These things I have spoken to you, that my joy might remain in you, and that your joy might be full.

12 This is my commandment, That you love one another, as I have loved you.

13 Greater love has no man than this, that a man lay down his life for his friends.

14 You are my friends, if you do whatever I command you.

15 From now on I do not call you servants; for the servant does not know what his lord does: but I have called you friends; for all things that I have heard of my Father I have made known to you.

16 You have not chosen me, but I have chosen you, and ordained you, that you should go and bring forth fruit, and that your fruit should remain: that whatever you shall ask of the Father in my name, he may give it to you.

17 These things I command you, that you love one another.

18 If the world hates you, you know that it hated me before it hated you.

19 If you were of the world, the world would love its own: but because you are not of the world, but I have chosen you out of the world, therefore the world hates you.

20 Remember the word that I said to you, The servant is not greater than his lord. If they have persecuted me, they will also persecute you; if they have kept my saying, they will keep yours also.

21 But all these things they will do to you for my name's sake, because they do not know him who sent me.

22 If I had not come and spoken to them, they would have no sin: but now they have no excuse for their sin.

23 He who hates me hates my Father also.

· ·

15:13 This is what Jesus did for humanity. He laid down His life so that we could live, proving God's love for us.

15:14 If we refuse to obey Him, we remain His enemies: "You adulterers and adulteresses, do you not know that the friendship of the world is enmity with God? whoever therefore will be a friend of the world is the enemy of God" (James 4:4).

24 If I had not done among them the works which no other man did, they would have no sin: but now they have both seen and hated both me and my Father.

25 But this comes to pass, that the word might be fulfilled that is written in their law, They hated me without a cause.

26 But when the Comforter has come, whom I will send to you from the Father, even the Spirit of truth, which proceeds from the Father, he shall testify of me:

27 And you also shall bear witness, because you have been with me from the beginning.

• •

15:23   No man can say he loves God but rejects Jesus Christ. See John 16:2,3.

CHAPTER 16

The Pain of Birth

THESE things have I spoken to you, that you should not be offended.

2 They shall put you out of the synagogues: yes, the time comes, that whoever kills you will think that he does God service.

3 And these things they will do to you, because they have not known the Father, nor me.

4 But these things I have told you, that when the time shall come, you may remember that I told you of them. And these things I did not say to you at the beginning, because I was with you.

5 But now I go my way to him who sent me; and none of you asks me, Where are you going?

6 But because I have said these things to you, sorrow has filled your heart.

7 Nevertheless I tell you the truth; It is expedient for you that I go away: for if I do not go away, the Comforter will not come to you; but if I depart, I will send him to you.

8 And when he has come, he will reprove the world of sin, and of righteousness, and of judgment:

9 Of sin, because they do not believe on me;

10 Of righteousness, because I go to my Father, and you see me no more;

11 Of judgment, because the prince of this world is judged.

12 I have yet many things to say to you, but you cannot bear them now.

13 However when he, the Spirit of truth, has come, he will guide you into all truth: for he shall not speak of himself; but whatever he shall hear, that shall he speak: and he will show you things to come.

14 He shall glorify me: for he shall receive of mine, and shall

show it to you.

15 All things that the Father has are mine: therefore I said that he shall take of mine, and shall show it to you.

16 A little while, and you shall not see me: and again, a little while, and you shall see me, because I go to the Father.

17 Then some of his disciples said among themselves, What is this that he said to us, A little while, and you shall not see me: and again, a little while, and you shall see me: and, Because I go to the Father?

18 They said therefore, What is this that he says, A little while? we cannot tell what he says.

19 Now Jesus knew that they were desirous to ask him, and said to them, Do you inquire among yourselves about what I said, A little while, and you shall not see me: and again, a little while, and you shall see me?

20 Verily, verily, I say to you, That you shall weep and lament, but the world shall rejoice: and you shall be sorrowful, but your sorrow shall be turned into joy.

21 A woman when she is in labor has sorrow, because her hour has come: but as soon as she has delivered the child, she remembers no more the anguish, for joy that a child is born into the

· ·

16:20   This is an obvious reference to the horror of the cross, and the unspeakable joy of the resurrection. How could anyone in his right mind look at the New Testament and say that Jesus was merely an example of a good human being? He is here graphically describing future events, something He *continually* did. The best of humanity cannot tell what the future holds. We can't even accurately predict tomorrow's weather, let alone *events* that will take place in the future. For those skeptics who may say that Jesus predicted *short-term* events and then manipulated situations so that they would be fulfilled, here are some of His long-term predictions (what would happen in the "latter days"—the end of the age) from Matthew 24 and Luke 21:

> There will be false Christs; wars and rumors of wars; nation rising against nation; famines; disease (pestilence); false prophets who will deceive many; and lawlessness (a forsaking of the Ten Commandments). The gospel will be preached in all the world. There will be great earthquakes in various places; signs from heaven (in the sun, moon, and stars); and persecution against Christians in all nations. Jesus warned that the sign to look for was the repossession of Jerusalem by the Jews. That happened in 1967, after 2,000 years, bringing into culmination all the signs of the times.

world.

22 And you now therefore have sorrow: but I will see you again, and your heart shall rejoice, and your joy no man will take from you.

23 And in that day you shall ask me nothing. Verily, verily, I say to you, Whatever you shall ask the Father in my name, he will give you.

24 Until now you have asked nothing in my name: ask, and you shall receive, that your joy may be full.

25 These things I have spoken to you in proverbs: but the time comes when I shall no longer speak to you in proverbs, but I shall show you plainly of the Father.

26 At that day you shall ask in my name: and I do not say to you, that I will pray the Father for you:

27 For the Father himself loves you, because you have loved me, and have believed that I came out from God.

28 I came forth from the Father, and have come into the world: again, I leave the world, and go to the Father.

29 His disciples said to him, Lo, now you speak plainly, and speak no proverb.

30 Now are we sure that you know all things, and do not need that any man should ask you; by this we believe that you came forth from God.

31 Jesus answered them, Do you now believe?

32 Behold, the hour comes, yes, has now come, that you shall be scattered, every man to his own, and shall leave me alone: and yet I am not alone, because the Father is with me.

33 These things I have spoken to you, that in me you might have peace. In the world you shall have tribulation: but be of good cheer; I have overcome the world.

· ·

16:33 These can only be the words of God.

CHAPTER 17

The Evil One

JESUS spoke these words and lifted up his eyes to heaven, and said, Father, the hour has come; glorify your Son, that your Son also may glorify you:

2 As you have given him power over all flesh, that he should give eternal life to as many as you have given him.

3 And this is life eternal, that they might know you the only true God, and Jesus Christ, whom you have sent.

4 I have glorified you on the earth: I have finished the work which you gave me to do.

5 And now, O Father, glorify me with your own self with the glory which I had with you before the world was.

6 I have manifested your name to the men which you gave me out of the world: they were yours, and you gave them to me; and they have kept your word.

7 Now they have known that all things whatever you have given me are of you.

8 For I have given to them the words which you gave me; and they have received them, and have known surely that I came out from you, and they have believed that you did send me.

9 I pray for them: I pray not for the world, but for those whom you have given me; for they are yours.

• •

17:1 Here we are given an intimate look at the words of prayer that Jesus uttered before He went to the cross. Again, this is the "hour" for which He was born.

17:3 Salvation doesn't come merely from knowing *about* God. Eternal life comes only through *knowing* Jesus Christ, the Son of God, personally through faith in Him.

17:5 This is another reference to Jesus' preexistence.

10 And all mine are yours, and yours are mine; and I am glorified in them.

11 And now I am no longer in the world, but these are in the world, and I come to you. Holy Father, keep through your own name those whom you have given me, that they may be one, as we are.

12 While I was with them in the world, I kept them in your name: those whom you gave me I have kept, and none of them is lost but the son of perdition; that the scripture might be fulfilled.

13 And now I come to you; and these things I speak in the world, that they might have my joy fulfilled in themselves.

14 I have given them your word; and the world has hated them, because they are not of the world, even as I am not of the world.

15 I do not pray that you should take them out of the world, but that you should keep them from the evil.

16 They are not of the world, even as I am not of the world.

17 Sanctify them through your truth: your word is truth.

18 As you have sent me into the world, even so I have also sent them into the world.

19 And for their sakes I sanctify myself, that they also might be sanctified through the truth.

20 Neither do I pray for these alone, but also for those who shall believe on me through their word;

21 That they all may be one; as you, Father, are in me, and I in you, that they also may be one in us: that the world may believe that you have sent me.

22 And the glory which you gave me I have given them; that they may be one, even as we are one:

23 I in them, and you in me, that they may be made perfect in one; and that the world may know that you have sent me, and have loved them, as you have loved me.

24 Father, I desire that they also, whom you have given me, may be with me where I am; that they may behold my glory, which you have given me: for you loved me before the foundation of the world.

25 O righteous Father, the world has not known you: but I have known you, and these have known that you have sent me.

26 And I have declared to them your name, and will declare it: that the love with which you have loved me may be in them, and I in them.

CHAPTER 18

Arrested

WHEN Jesus had spoken these words, he went forth with his disciples over the brook Cedron, where there was a garden, into which he and his disciples entered.

2 And Judas also, who betrayed him, knew the place: for Jesus often resorted there with his disciples.

3 Judas then, having received a band of men and officers from the chief priests and Pharisees, came there with lanterns and torches and weapons.

4 Jesus therefore, knowing all things that should come upon him, went forth and said to them, Whom do you seek?

5 They answered him, Jesus of Nazareth. Jesus said to them, I am he. And Judas also, who betrayed him, stood with them.

6 Then as soon as he had said to them, I am he, they went backward, and fell to the ground.

7 Then he asked them again, Whom do you seek? And they said, Jesus of Nazareth.

8 Jesus answered, I have told you that I am he: if therefore you seek me, let these go their way:

9 That the saying might be fulfilled, which he spoke, Of them which you gave me I have lost none.

10 Then Simon Peter having a sword drew it, and struck the high priest's servant, and cut off his right ear. The servant's name was Malchus.

11 Then Jesus said to Peter, Put up your sword into the sheath: the cup which my Father has given me, shall I not drink it?

12 Then the band and the captain and officers of the Jews took Jesus, and bound him,

13 And led him away to Annas first; for he was father-in-law to Caiaphas, who was the high priest that same year.

14 Now Caiaphas was he who gave counsel to the Jews, that it was expedient that one man should die for the people.

15 And Simon Peter followed Jesus, and so did another disciple: that disciple was known to the high priest, and went in with Jesus into the palace of the high priest.

16 But Peter stood at the door outside. Then that other disciple, who was known to the high priest, went out and spoke to her who kept the door, and brought in Peter.

17 Then the damsel who kept the door said to Peter, Are you not also one of this man's disciples? He said, I am not.

18 And the servants and officers stood there, who had made a fire of coals; for it was cold: and they warmed themselves: and Peter stood with them and warmed himself.

19 The high priest then asked Jesus of his disciples, and of his doctrine.

20 Jesus answered him, I spoke openly to the world; I always taught in the synagogue and in the temple, where the Jews always resort; and in secret I have said nothing.

21 Why do you ask me? ask those who heard me what I have said to them: behold, they know what I said.

22 And when he had thus spoken, one of the officers who stood by struck Jesus with the palm of his hand, saying, Do you answer the high priest so?

23 Jesus answered him, If I have spoken evil, bear witness of the evil: but if well, why do you strike me?

24 Now Annas had sent him bound to Caiaphas the high priest.

25 And Simon Peter stood and warmed himself. Therefore they said to him, Are you not also one of his disciples? He denied it and said, I am not.

26 One of the servants of the high priest, being his kinsman whose ear Peter cut off, said, Did I not see you in the garden with him?

27 Peter then denied again: and immediately the cock crowed.

28 Then they led Jesus from Caiaphas to the hall of judgment: and it was early; and they themselves did not go into the judgment hall, lest they should be defiled; but that they might eat the Passover.

29 Pilate then went out to them, and said, What accusation do you bring against this man?

30 They answered and said to him, If he were not a malefactor,

we would not have delivered him up to you.

31 Then Pilate said to them, You take him, and judge him according to your law. The Jews therefore said to him, It is not lawful for us to put any man to death:

32 That the saying of Jesus might be fulfilled, which he spoke, signifying what death he should die.

33 Then Pilate entered into the judgment hall again, and called Jesus, and said to him, Are you the King of the Jews?

34 Jesus answered him, Do you say this thing of yourself, or did others tell it of me?

35 Pilate answered, Am I a Jew? Your own nation and the chief priests have delivered you to me: what have you done?

36 Jesus answered, My kingdom is not of this world: if my kingdom were of this world, then my servants would fight, that I should not be delivered to the Jews: but now my kingdom is not from here.

37 Pilate therefore said to him, Are you a king then? Jesus answered, You say that I am a king. To this end I was born, and for this cause I came into the world, that I should bear witness to the truth. Everyone who is of the truth hears my voice.

38 Pilate said to him, What is truth? And when he had said this, he went out again to the Jews, and said to them, I find in him no fault at all.

39 But you have a custom, that I should release to you one at the Passover: do you therefore want me to release to you the King of the Jews?

40 Then they all cried again, saying, Not this man, but Barabbas. Now Barabbas was a robber.

. . . .

18:37 Do you "hear" His voice?

18:38 It seems that Pilate's question was rhetorical. The Truth stood before him in human form (see John 14:6), which he refused to recognize. However, Pilate did recognize that Jesus was without fault.

18:38 The Lamb of God was perfect—without sin: "You were not redeemed with corruptible things, like silver and gold, from your aimless conduct received by tradition from your fathers; but with the precious blood of Christ, as of a lamb without blemish and without spot. He indeed was foreordained before the foundation of the world, but was manifest in these last times for you, who through him do believe in God, who raised him up from the dead and gave him glory; that your faith and hope might be in God" (1 Peter 1:18–21).

CHAPTER 19

Murdered

T HEN Pilate therefore took Jesus, and scourged him.
  2 And the soldiers twisted a crown of thorns, and put it on his head, and they put on him a purple robe,

3 And said, Hail, King of the Jews! and they struck him with their hands.

. . . .

19:1 The following is from Isaiah 53, written approximately 700 B.C. Look at how graphically it describes the suffering Messiah:

"Who has believed our report? and to whom is the arm of the Lord revealed? For he shall grow up before him as a tender plant, and as a root out of a dry ground: he has no form or comeliness; and when we see him, there is no beauty that we should desire him. He is despised and rejected of men; a man of sorrows and acquainted with grief: and we hid, as it were, our faces from him; he was despised, and we did not esteem him. Surely he has borne our griefs and carried our sorrows: yet we esteemed him stricken, smitten of God, and afflicted. But he was wounded for our transgressions, he was bruised for our iniquities: the chastisement of our peace was upon him; and with his stripes we are healed.

"All we like sheep have gone astray; we have turned, every one, to his own way; and the Lord has laid on him the iniquity of us all. He was oppressed and he was afflicted, yet he opened not his mouth: he was brought as a lamb to the slaughter, and as a sheep before its shearers is dumb, so he opened not his mouth. He was taken from prison and from judgment: and who shall declare his generation? for he was cut off out of the land of the living: for the transgression of my people he was stricken. And he made his grave with the wicked, and with the rich in his death; because he had done no violence, neither was any deceit in his mouth.

"Yet it pleased the Lord to bruise him; he has put him to grief: when

4 Pilate therefore went forth again, and said to them, Behold, I bring him forth to you, that you may know that I find no fault in him.

5 Then Jesus came forth, wearing the crown of thorns and the purple robe. And Pilate said to them, Behold the man!

6 Therefore when the chief priests and officers saw him, they cried out, saying, Crucify him, crucify him. Pilate said to them, You take him, and crucify him: for I find no fault in him.

7 The Jews answered him, We have a law, and by our law he ought to die, because he made himself the Son of God.

8 When Pilate therefore heard that saying, he was the more afraid;

9 And went again into the judgment hall, and said to Jesus, Where are you from? But Jesus gave him no answer.

10 Then Pilate said to him, Do you not speak to me? Do you not know that I have power to crucify you, and have power to release you?

11 Jesus answered, You could have no power at all against me, except it were given you from above: therefore he who delivered me to you has the greater sin.

12 And from then on Pilate sought to release him: but the Jews cried out, saying, If you let this man go, you are not Caesar's friend: whoever makes himself a king speaks against Caesar.

13 When Pilate therefore heard that saying, he brought Jesus forth, and sat down in the judgment seat in a place that is called the Pavement, but in the Hebrew, Gabbatha.

14 And it was the preparation of the Passover, and about the sixth hour: and he said to the Jews, Behold your King!

· ·

you make his soul an offering for sin, he shall see his seed, he shall prolong his days, and the pleasure of the Lord shall prosper in his hand. He shall see of the travail of his soul, and shall be satisfied: by his knowledge my righteous servant shall justify many; for he shall bear their iniquities. Therefore I will divide him a portion with the great, and he shall divide the spoil with the strong; because he has poured out his soul unto death: and he was numbered with the transgressors; and he bore the sin of many, and made intercession for the transgressors."

19:8 You have the same dilemma. If Jesus was who He said He was, you must obey His words or you will be damned for eternity. Think about that for a moment. Like Pilate, you *should* be afraid.

19:14 This occurred at noon.

15 But they cried out, Away with him, away with him, crucify him. Pilate said to them, Shall I crucify your King? The chief priest answered, We have no king but Caesar.

16 Then he delivered him therefore to them to be crucified. And they took Jesus, and led him away.

17 And he bearing his cross went forth into a place called the place of a skull, which is called in the Hebrew Golgotha:

18 Where they crucified him, and two others with him, one on either side, and Jesus in the midst.

19 And Pilate wrote a title, and put it on the cross. And the writing was, JESUS OF NAZARETH THE KING OF THE JEWS.

20 Then many of the Jews read this title: for the place where Jesus was crucified was near to the city: and it was written in Hebrew, and Greek, and Latin.

21 Then the chief priests of the Jews said to Pilate, Do not write, The King of the Jews; but that he said, I am King of the Jews.

22 Pilate answered, What I have written I have written.

23 Then the soldiers, when they had crucified Jesus, took his garments and made four parts, to every soldier a part; and also his coat: now the coat was without seam, woven from the top throughout.

24 Therefore they said among themselves, Let us not tear it, but cast lots for it, whose it shall be: that the scripture might be fulfilled, which says, They divided my garments among them, and for my clothing they did cast lots. Therefore these things the soldiers did.

25 Now there stood by the cross of Jesus his mother, and his mother's sister, Mary the wife of Cleophas, and Mary Magdalene.

26 When Jesus therefore saw his mother, and the disciple whom he loved standing by, he said to his mother, Woman, behold your son!

27 Then he said to the disciple, Behold your mother! And from that hour that disciple took her to his own home.

28 After this, Jesus knowing that all things were now accomplished, that the scripture might be fulfilled, said, I thirst.

29 Now there was set a vessel full of vinegar: and they filled a sponge with vinegar, and put it upon hyssop, and put it to his mouth.

30 When Jesus therefore had received the vinegar, he said, It is finished: and he bowed his head, and gave up his spirit.

31 The Jews therefore, because it was the preparation, that the bodies should not remain upon the cross on the Sabbath day (for that Sabbath day was a high day), asked Pilate that their legs might be broken, and that they might be taken away.

32 Then the soldiers came and broke the legs of the first, and of

• •

19:28   Look at Psalm 22, written approximately 1,000 B.C.:

"My God, my God, why have you forsaken me? why are you so far from helping me, and from the words of my groaning?...I am a worm, and no man; a reproach of men, and despised of the people. All those who see me laugh me to scorn: they shoot out the lip, they shake the head, saying, He trusted on the Lord that he would deliver him: let him deliver him, seeing he delighted in him. But you are he who took me out of the womb: you made me trust when I was upon my mother's breasts. I was cast upon you from birth: you are my God from my mother's womb. Be not far from me; for trouble is near; for there is none to help. Many bulls have surrounded me: strong bulls of Bashan have encompassed me. They gape upon me with their mouths, as a raging and roaring lion. I am poured out like water, and all my bones are out of joint: my heart is like wax; it is melted within me. My strength is dried up like a potsherd; and my tongue clings to my jaws; you have brought me to the dust of death. For dogs have surrounded me: the assembly of the wicked has enclosed me: they pierced my hands and my feet. I can count all my

bones. They look and stare upon me. They divide my garments among them, and cast lots for my clothing."

Psalm 22 was clearly fulfilled in the crucifixion of Jesus of Nazareth. He was aware of their scorn; He could hear the mocking words; He was praying; the strain of crucifixion pulled His bones out of joint; loss of blood made His heart feel as though it were melting; His strength completely left Him; thirst caused His tongue to adhere to His mouth; they pierced His hands and feet; He could see them gambling for His clothes. This is what He suffered so that you could be forgiven. Is it nothing to you? Is your heart made of stone? Humble yourself and cry out, "What love you have for a wretch like me. What amazing grace You expressed through the cross. Forgive me for transgressing Your Law. Create a clean heart in me, O God."

19:29   This is a fulfillment of a prophecy in Psalm 69:21: "They also gave me gall for my food; and in my thirst they gave me vinegar to drink."

the other who was crucified with him.

33 But when they came to Jesus, and saw that he was dead already, they did not break his legs:

34 But one of the soldiers with a spear pierced his side, and immediately out came blood and water.

35 And he that saw it bore record, and his record is true: and he knows what he said is true, that you might believe.

36 For these things were done that the scripture should be fulfilled, Not a bone of him shall be broken.

37 And again another scripture says, They shall look on him

· ·

19:30 "It is finished" signified that, by shedding His blood for mankind, the debt for sin had been paid. The demands of the Law had been satisfied. Perhaps you know that sin is wrong, but you don't feel sorry for it. You enjoy it and it seems okay as long as it doesn't hurt anyone. Here's an analogy that may help. A child was forbidden to touch his father's antique $25,000 vase. One day the child disobeyed his father and broke it. However, he believed the vase was merely worth $2, so he wasn't too concerned. He could easily replace it. It was only when he was later told of its true value that he saw the seriousness of his transgression and felt sorrow of heart. It was the knowledge of the solemn nature of breaking an expensive antique (which he had been told not to touch) that enabled him to feel sorrow. If he had been left in ignorance of the value of the vase, he wouldn't have been truly sorry. Would you be upset if you had broken a vase that you could easily replace? Again, when he understood the expense to which his father would have to go to make things right, he was able to see the seriousness of his transgression and thus feel genuine sorrow of heart.

It is true that sin is pleasurable. It is true that we don't see anything too serious about lust, white lies, etc. So how then can we be sorry for "trivialities"? Here's how. Look at what it cost the Father to make things right. Look to the battered and bruised body of the Son of God, as His soul was made an offering for sin. The Bible says that He was more marred than any man, that He was hardly recognizable as a human being as He hung on the cross and took the punishment for your sins. If you can't feel sorry in the face of such horror, then get on your knees and cry out for God to take away your heart of stone. Ask Him to show you your sins as He sees them. Ask Him to give you a vision of the cross. He may just do that.

19:31 When the legs were broken, the victim could no longer lift himself up to breathe and therefore suffocated.

19:36 This again pictures Jesus as the sacrificial Lamb (see John 1:29). Just as the Passover lamb was not to have any bones broken (Numbers 9:12), neither did Jesus, the Lamb of God who was slain to take away the sin of the world.

whom they pierced.

38 And after this Joseph of Arimathaea, being a disciple of Jesus, but secretly for fear of the Jews, asked Pilate that he might take away the body of Jesus: and Pilate gave him permission. He came therefore, and took the body of Jesus.

39 And Nicodemus, who at first came to Jesus by night, also came and brought a mixture of myrrh and aloes, about a hundred pounds.

40 Then they took the body of Jesus, and wound it in linen clothes with the spices, as the manner of the Jews is to bury.

· ·

19:37 This is a fulfillment of a prophecy in Zechariah 12:10.

19:40 The Hands of the Carpenter. It was Joseph of Arimathaea who had the honor of taking the body of Jesus down from the cross. Think what it would be like to have to pull the thick, barbed Roman nails from the cold and lifeless hands of the Son of God. These were carpenter's hands, which once held nails and wood, now being held by nails and wood. These were the hands that broke bread and fed multitudes, now being broken to feed multitudes. They once applied clay to a blind man's eyes, touched lepers, healed the sick, washed the disciples' feet, and took children in His arms. These were the hands that, more than once, loosed the cold hand of death, now held firmly by its icy grip. These were the fingers that wrote in the sand when the adulterous woman was cast at His feet, and for the love of God, fashioned a whip that purged His Father's house. These were the same fingers that took bread and dipped it in a dish, and gave it to Judas as a gesture of deep love and friendship. Here was the Bread of Life itself, being dipped in the cup of suffering, as the ultimate gesture of God's love for the evil world that Judas represented.

Joseph's shame, that he had been afraid to own the Savior, sickened him as he tore the blood-sodden feet from the six-inch cold steel spikes that fastened them to the cross. These were the "beautiful feet" of Him who preached the gospel of peace, that Mary washed with her hair, that walked upon the Sea of Galilee, now crimson with a sea of blood. As Joseph reached out his arms to get Him down from the cross, perhaps he stared for an instant at the inanimate face of the Son of God. His heart wrenched as he looked upon Him whom they had pierced. This face, which once radiated with the glory of God on the Mount of Transfiguration, which so many had looked upon with such veneration, was now blood-stained from the needle-sharp crown of thorns, deathly pale and twisted from unspeakable suffering as the sin of the world was laid upon Him.

His eyes, which once sparkled with the life of God, now stared at nothingness, as He was brought into the dust of death. His lips, which spoke such gracious words and calmed the fears of so many, were swollen and bruised from the beating given to Him by the hardened fists of cruel soldiers. As it is written,

41 Now in the place where he was crucified there was a garden; and in the garden a new tomb, in which a man was never yet laid.
42 Therefore, there they laid Jesus because of the Jews' preparation day; for the tomb was nearby.

• •

"His visage was so marred more than any man" (Isaiah 52:14).

Nicodemus may have reached up to help Joseph with the body. As the cold blood of the Lamb of God covered his hand, perhaps he was reminded of the blood of the Passover lamb he had seen shed so many times. The death of each spotless animal had been so quick and merciful, but this death had been unspeakably cruel, vicious, inhumane, and brutal. It seemed that all the hatred that sin-loving humanity had for the Light formed itself into a dark and evil spear, and was thrust with cruel delight into the perfect Lamb of God.

Perhaps as he carefully pried the crown from His head, looked at the gaping hole in His side, the deep mass of abrasions upon His back, and the mutilated wounds in His hands and feet, a sense of outrage engrossed him, that this could happen to such a Man as this. But the words of the prophet Isaiah rang within his heart:

> "He was wounded for our transgressions, he was bruised for our iniquities . . . the Lord has laid on him the iniquity of us all . . . as a lamb to the slaughter . . . for the transgression of my people he was stricken . . . yet it pleased the Lord to bruise him . . . by his knowledge shall my righteous servant justify many" (Isaiah 53:5–11).

Jesus of Nazareth was stripped of His robe, that we might be robed in pure righteousness. He suffered a deathly thirst, that our thirst for life might be quenched. He agonized under the curse of the Law, that we might relish the blessing of the gospel. He took upon Himself the hatred of the world, so that we could experience the love of God. Hell was let loose upon Him so that heaven could be let loose upon us. Jesus of Nazareth tasted the bitterness of death, so that we might taste the sweetness of life everlasting. The Son of God willingly passed over His life, that death might freely pass over the sons and daughters of Adam.

May Calvary's cross be as real to us as it was to those who stood on its bloody soil on that terrible day. May we also gaze upon the face of the crucified Son of God, and may shame grip our hearts if ever the fear of man comes near our souls. May we identify with the apostle Paul, who whispered in awe of God's great love: "God forbid that I should glory, except in the cross of our Lord Jesus Christ, by whom the world is crucified unto me, and I unto the world" (Galatians 6:14).

CHAPTER 20

After Three Days

THE first day of the week Mary Magdalene came early, when it was yet dark, to the tomb, and saw the stone taken away from the tomb.

2 Then she ran and came to Simon Peter, and to the other disciple, whom Jesus loved, and said to them, They have taken away the Lord out of the tomb, and we do not know where they have laid him.

3 Peter therefore went forth, and that other disciple, and came to the tomb.

4 So they both ran together: and the other disciple outran Peter and came first to the tomb.

5 And he, stooping down, and looking in, saw the linen clothes lying; yet he did not go in.

6 Then Simon Peter came following him, and went into the tomb, and saw the linen clothes lie,

7 And the cloth that was about his head, not lying with the linen clothes, but wrapped together in a place by itself.

8 Then that other disciple, who came first to the tomb, went in also, and he saw and believed.

9 For as yet they did not know the scripture, that he must rise again from the dead.

10 Then the disciples went away again to their own home.

11 But Mary stood outside at the tomb weeping: and as she wept, she stooped down and looked into the tomb,

12 And saw two angels in white sitting, one at the head and the other at the feet, where the body of Jesus had lain.

13 And they said to her, Woman, why are you weeping? She said to them, Because they have taken away my Lord, and I do not know where they have laid him.

14 And when she had said this, she turned herself back and saw Jesus standing, and did not know that it was Jesus.

15 Jesus said to her, Woman, why are you weeping? whom do you seek? She, supposing him to be the gardener, said to him, Sir, if you have carried him from here, tell me where you have laid him, and I will take him away.

16 Jesus said to her, Mary. She turned herself, and said to him, Rabboni; which is to say, Master.

17 Jesus said to her, Do not touch me; for I have not yet ascended to my Father: but go to my brethren and say to them, I ascend to my Father, and your Father; and to my God, and your God.

18 Mary Magdalene came and told the disciples that she had seen the Lord, and that he had spoken these things to her.

19 Then the same day at evening, being the first day of the week, when the doors were shut where the disciples were assembled for fear of the Jews, Jesus came and stood in the midst, and said to them, Peace be to you.

20 And when he had said this, he showed to them his hands and his side. Then the disciples were glad, when they saw the Lord.

21 Then Jesus said to them again, Peace be to you: as my Father has sent me, even so I send you.

22 And when he had said this, he breathed on them, and said to them, Receive the Holy Spirit:

23 If you forgive the sins of any, they are forgiven them; and if you retain the sins of any, they are retained.

24 But Thomas, one of the twelve, called Didymus, was not with them when Jesus came.

25 The other disciples therefore said to him, We have seen the Lord. But he said to them, Except I shall see in his hands the print of the nails, and put my finger into the print of the nails, and thrust my hand into his side, I will not believe.

. . . .

20:16   God also knows you by name. He knows how many hairs are on your head, and every thought of your heart. Nothing is hidden from His eyes. That will be a source of comfort to you if you have peace with Him through the cross. If you don't have peace with Him, that thought should terrify you.

20:25   Thomas was guilty of the sin of unbelief (calling God a liar; see 1 John 5:10). How could we ever doubt the fact that Jesus Christ is Lord? He is the King of kings and the Lord of lords. Thank God that we have this insightful testimony of Scripture, this wonderful book called the Gospel of John.

26 And after eight days again his disciples were inside, and Thomas with them: then Jesus came, the doors being shut, and stood in the midst and said, Peace be to you.

27 Then he said to Thomas, Reach here your finger, and behold my hands; and reach here your hand, and thrust it into my side: and do not be faithless, but believing.

28 And Thomas answered and said to him, My Lord and my God.

29 Jesus said to him, Thomas, because you have seen me, you have believed: blessed are those who have not seen, and yet have believed.

30 And truly Jesus did many other signs in the presence of his disciples, which are not written in this book:

31 But these are written, that you might believe that Jesus is the Christ, the Son of God; and that believing you might have life through his name.

• •

20:31 The Gospel of John was written for the sole purpose of your salvation —that by placing your trust in Jesus Christ you will receive eternal life. Did it accomplish its goal?

CHAPTER 21

His Testimony is True

A FTER these things Jesus showed himself again to the disciples at the sea of Tiberias; and in this way he showed himself.

2 There were together Simon Peter, and Thomas called Didymus, and Nathanael of Cana in Galilee, and the sons of Zebedee, and two of his other disciples.

3 Simon Peter said to them, I am going fishing. They said to him, We also are going with you. They went forth, and entered into a ship immediately; and that night they caught nothing.

4 But when the morning had come, Jesus stood on the shore: but the disciples did not know that it was Jesus.

5 Then Jesus said to them, Children, have you any food? They answered him, No.

6 And he said to them, Cast the net on the right side of the ship, and you shall find. They cast therefore, and now they were not able to draw it for the multitude of fishes.

7 Therefore that disciple whom Jesus loved said to Peter, It is the Lord. Now when Simon Peter heard that it was the Lord, he put on his outer garment (for he had removed it), and cast himself into the sea.

8 And the other disciples came in a little ship (for they were not far from land, but as it were two hundred cubits), dragging the net with fishes.

9 Then as soon as they had come to land, they saw a fire of coals there, and fish laid on it, and bread.

10 Jesus said to them, Bring some of the fish which you have now caught.

11 Simon Peter went up, and drew the net to land full of great fishes, a hundred and fifty and three: and although there were so many, yet the net was not broken.

12 Jesus said to them, Come and dine. And none of the disciples dared ask him, Who are you? knowing that it was the Lord.

13 Jesus then came and took bread, and gave, and likewise the fish.

14 This is now the third time that Jesus showed himself to his

• •

21:14   Here is another account of Jesus' appearing after the resurrection (from the Book of Luke):

"And, behold, two of them went that same day to a village called Emmaus, which was from Jerusalem about threescore furlongs [seven miles]. And they talked together of all these things which had happened. And it came to pass, that, while they communed together and reasoned, Jesus himself drew near and went with them. But their eyes were restrained so that they did not know him. And he said to them, What manner of communications are these that you have with one another, as you walk and are sad? And one of them, whose name was Cleopas, answering said to him, Are you only a stranger in Jerusalem, and have not known the things which have come to pass there in these days? And he said to them, What things? And they said to him, Concerning Jesus of Nazareth, who was a prophet mighty in deed and word before God and all the people: and how the chief priests and our rulers delivered him to be condemned to death, and have crucified him. But we were hoping that it was he who would redeem Israel: and beside all this, today is the third day since these things happened. Yes, and certain women of our company made us astonished, who arrived early at the tomb; and when they did not find his body, they came saying that they had also seen a vision of angels who said that he was alive. And certain of those who were with us went to the tomb and found it even as the women had said: but him they did not see.

"Then he said to them, O fools, and slow of heart to believe all that the prophets have spoken: Ought not the Christ to have suffered these things, and to enter into his glory? And beginning at Moses and all the prophets, he expounded to them in all the scriptures the things concerning himself. And they drew near to the village where they were going: and he made as though he would have gone further. But they constrained him, saying, Abide with us: for it is toward evening and the day is far spent. And he went in to stay with them. And it came to pass, as he sat at the table with

disciples, after he was risen from the dead.

15 So when they had dined, Jesus said to Simon Peter, Simon, son of Jonah, do you love me more than these? He said to him, Yes, Lord; you know that I love you. He said to him, Feed my lambs.

16 He said to him again the second time, Simon, son of Jonah, do you love me? He said to him, Yes, Lord; you know that I love you. He said to him, Feed my sheep.

17 He said to him the third time, Simon, son of Jonah, do you love me? Peter was grieved because he said to him the third time, Do you love me? And he said to him, Lord, you know all things; you know that I love you. Jesus said to him, Feed my sheep.

18 Verily, verily, I say to you, When you were young, you girded yourself, and walked where you wished: but when you shall be old, you shall stretch forth your hands, and another shall gird you, and carry you where you do not wish.

19 This he spoke, signifying by what death he should glorify God. And when he had spoken this, he said to him, Follow me.

20 Then Peter, turning about, saw the disciple whom Jesus loved following; who also leaned on his breast at supper and said, Lord, who is he that betrays you?

21 Peter seeing him said to Jesus, Lord, and what shall this man do?

22 Jesus said to him, If I will that he remain till I come, what is that to you? You follow me.

23 Then this saying went out among the brethren, that that disciple should not die: yet Jesus did not say to him, He shall not die; but, If I will that he remain till I come, what is that to you?

24 This is the disciple who testifies of these things, and wrote these things: and we know that his testimony is true.

25 And there are also many other things which Jesus did, which, if they should be written every one, I suppose that even the world itself could not contain the books that should be written. Amen.

. . . .

them, that he took bread, and blessed and broke it, and gave it to them. And their eyes were opened, and they knew him; and he vanished out of their sight. And they said to one another, Did not our heart burn within us, while he talked with us by the way, and while he opened the scriptures to us?" (Luke 24:13–32).

The Ten Commandments

You shall have no other gods before Me.

You shall not make to yourself any graven image.

You shall not take the name of the
LORD your God in vain.

Remember the Sabbath day, to keep it holy.

Honor your father and your mother.

You shall not kill.

You shall not commit adultery.

You shall not steal.

You shall not bear false witness against
your neighbor.

You shall not covet.

(EXODUS 20:1–17)

Principles of Christian Growth

1. Feeding on the Word—Daily Nutrition

A healthy baby has a healthy appetite. If you have truly been "born" of the Spirit of God, you *will* have a healthy appetite. The Bible says, "As newborn babes, desire the pure milk of the word, that you may grow thereby" (1 Peter 2:2). Feed yourself daily without fail. Job said, "I have esteemed the words of His mouth more than my necessary food" (Job 23:12). The more you eat, the quicker you will grow, and the less bruising you will have. Speed up the process and save yourself some pain—vow to read God's Word every day, *without fail.* Say to yourself, "No Bible, no breakfast. No read, no feed." Be like Job, and put your Bible *before* your belly. If you do that, God promises that you will be like a fruitful, strong, and healthy tree (Psalm 1). Each day, find somewhere quiet and thoroughly soak your soul in the Word of God.

There may be times when you read through its pages with great enthusiasm, and other times when it seems dry and even boring. But food profits your body whether you enjoy it or not. As a child, you no doubt ate desserts with great enthusiasm. Perhaps vegetables weren't so exciting. If you were a normal child, you probably had to be *encouraged* to eat them at first. Then, as you matured in life you disciplined yourself to eat vegetables, because they benefit you physically even though they may not bring pleasure to your taste buds.

2. Faith—Elevators Can Let You Down

When a young man once told me, "I find it hard to believe some of the things in the Bible," I smiled and asked, "What's your name?" When he said, "Paul," I casually answered, "I don't believe you." He looked at me questioningly. I repeated, "What's your name?" Again he said, "Paul," and again I answered, "I don't believe you." Then I asked, "Where do you live?" When he told me, I said, "I don't believe that either." You should have seen his reaction. He was angry. I said, "You look a little upset. Do you know why? You're upset because I didn't believe what you told me. If you tell me that your name is Paul, and I say, 'I don't believe you,' it means that I think you are a liar. You are trying to deceive me by telling me your name is Paul, when it's not."

Then I told him that if he, a mere man, felt insulted by my lack of faith in his word, how much more does he insult Almighty God by refusing to believe His Word. In doing so, he was saying that God isn't worth trusting—that He is a liar and a deceiver. The Bible says, "He who does not believe God has made him a liar" (1 John 5:10). It also says, "Take heed, brethren, least there be in any of you *an evil heart of unbelief…*" (Hebrews 3:12, emphasis added). Martin Luther said, "What greater insult… can there be to God, than not to believe His promises."

I have heard people say, "I just find it hard to have faith in God," not realizing the implications of their words. These are the same people who accept the daily weather forecast, believe the newspapers, and trust their lives to a pilot they have never seen whenever they board a plane. We exercise faith every day. We rely on our car's brakes. We trust history books, medical journals, and elevators. Yet elevators can let us down; history books can be wrong; planes can crash. How much more then should we trust the sure and true promises of Almighty God. He will never let us down… if we trust Him.

Cynics often argue, "You can't trust the Bible—it's full of mistakes." It is. The first mistake was when man rejected God, and the Scriptures show men and women making the same tragic mistake again and again. It's also full of what *seem to be* contradictions. For example, the Scriptures tell us that "with God nothing shall be impossible" (Luke 1:37); there is nothing Almighty God can't do. Yet we are also told that it is "impossible for God to lie" (Hebrews 6:18). So there is something God cannot do! Isn't that an obvious "mistake" in the Bible? No, it isn't.

Lying, deception, bearing false witness, etc., is so repulsive to God, so disgusting to Him, so against His holy character, that the

Scriptures draw on the strength of the word "impossible" to substantiate the claim. He cannot, could not, and would not lie.

That means that in a world where we are continually let down, we can totally rely on, trust in, and count on His promises. They are sure, certain, indisputable, true, trustworthy, reliable, faithful, unfailing, dependable, steadfast, and an anchor for the soul. In other words, you can truly believe them, and because of that, you can throw yourself blindfolded and without reserve into His mighty hands. He will *never, ever* let you down. Do you believe that?

3. Evangelism—Our Most Sobering Task

Late in December 1996, a large family gathered for a joyous Christmas. So many were gathered that night that five of the children slept in the converted garage, kept warm during the night by an electric heater placed near the door.

During the early hours of the morning, the heater suddenly burst into flames, blocking the doorway. In seconds the room became a blazing inferno. A frantic 911 call revealed the unspeakable terror as one of the children could be heard screaming, *"I'm on fire!"* The distraught father rushed into the flames to try to save his beloved children, receiving burns to 50% of his body. Tragically, all five children burned to death. They died because steel bars on the windows thwarted their escape. There was only one door, and it was blocked by the flames.

Imagine you're back in time, just minutes before the heater burst into flames. You peer through the darkness at the peaceful sight of five sleeping youngsters, knowing that at any moment the room will erupt into an inferno and burn the flesh of horrified children. *Can you in good conscience walk away?* No! You *must* awaken them and warn them to run from that death trap!

The world sleeps peacefully in the darkness of ignorance. There is only one Door by which they may escape death. The steel bars of sin prevent their salvation, and at the same time call for the flames of Eternal Justice. What a fearful thing Judgment Day will be! The fires of the wrath of Almighty God will burn for eternity. The Church has been entrusted with the task of awakening them before it's too late. We cannot turn our backs and walk away in complacency. *Think of how the father ran into the flames.* His love knew no bounds. Our devotion to the sober task God has given us will be in direct proportion to our love for the lost. There are only a few who run headlong into the flames to warn them to flee (Luke 10:2). *Please* be one of them. We really have no choice. The apostle Paul said, "Woe is me, if I do not preach the gospel!" (1 Corinthians 9:16).

The "Prince of Preachers," Charles Spurgeon, said, "We need to be ashamed at the bare suspicion of unconcern." A Christian *cannot* be apathetic about the salvation of the world. The love of God in him will motivate him to seek and save that which is lost.

You probably have a limited amount of time after your conversion to impact your unsaved friends and family with the gospel. After the initial shock of your conversion, they will put you in a neat little ribbon-tied box, and keep you at arm's length. So it's important that you take advantage of the short time you have while you still have their ears.

However, here's some advice that will save you a great deal of grief. As a new Christian, I did almost irreparable damage by acting like a wild bull in a crystal showroom. I bullied my mom, my dad, and many of my friends to try to get them to make a "decision for Christ." I was sincere, zealous, loving, kind, and stupid. I didn't understand that salvation doesn't come through making a "decision," but through repentance, and repentance is God-given (see 2 Timothy 2:25). The Bible teaches that no one can come to the Son unless the Father "draws" him. If you are able to get a decision but they have no conviction of sin, you will almost certainly end up with a still-born on your hands. Keep in mind that you are called to plant the seed of the gospel, so don't try to reap prematurely. Let God do His work in causing the seed to grow. Sometimes that takes time.

In my "zeal without knowledge" I actually inoculated the very ones I was so desperately trying to reach. There is nothing more important to you than the salvation of your loved ones, and you don't want to blow it. If you do, you may find that you don't have a second chance. Fervently pray for them, thanking God for their salvation. Let them *see* your faith. Let them *feel* your kindness, your genuine love, and your gentleness. Buy gifts for no reason. Do chores when you are not asked to. Go the extra mile. Put yourself in their position. You know that you have found everlasting life. *Death has lost its sting!* Your joy is unspeakable—but as far as they are concerned, you have been brainwashed. You have become part of a weird sect. So your loving actions will speak more loudly than ten thousand eloquent sermons.

It is because of these thoughts that you should hold back from verbal confrontation with your family until you have knowledge that will guide your zeal. To learn how to biblically share your faith, see *Revival's Golden Key* (for ordering information, see the Resources at the back of this book). Pray for wisdom and for a sensitivity to God's timing. You may have only one shot, so make it count. Keep your cool. If you don't, you may end up with a lifetime of regret. You often change friends, but you have to live with your family for a lifetime. *Believe* me, it is better to hear a loved one or a close friend say, "Tell me about your faith in Jesus Christ," rather than you saying, "Sit down. I want to talk to you."

We should share our faith with others *whenever* we can. The Bible says there are only two times we should do this: "in season, and out of season" (2 Timothy 4:2). The apostle Paul *pleaded* for prayer for his own personal witness. He said, "[Pray] for me, that utterance may be given to me, that I may open my mouth boldly to make known the mystery of the gospel, for which I am an ambassador in chains: that in it I may speak boldly, as I ought to speak" (Ephesians 6:19,20).

Remember that you have the sobering responsibility of speaking to other peoples' loved ones. Perhaps another Christian has prayed earnestly that God would use a faithful witness to speak to his beloved mom or dad, and *you* are the answer to that prayer. You are the true and faithful witness God wants to use.

Keep the fate of the ungodly before your eyes. Too many of us settle down on a padded pew and become introverted. Our world becomes a monastery without walls. Our friends are confined solely to those *within* the Church, when Jesus was the "friend of sinners." So take the time to deliberately befriend the lost for the sake of their salvation. Remember that each and every person who dies in his sins has an appointment with the Judge of the Universe. Hell opens wide its terrible jaws. There is no more so-

bering task than to be entrusted with the gospel of salvation—
working with God for the eternal well-being of dying humanity.

4. Prayer—"Wait for a Minute"

God always answers prayer. Sometimes He says yes; sometimes
He says no; and sometimes He says, "Wait for a minute." And
since God is outside of time and to Him a day is as a thousand
years (2 Peter 3:8), that could mean a ten-year wait for us. So ask
in faith, but rest in peace-filled patience.

Surveys show that more than 90% of Americans pray daily.
No doubt they pray for health, wealth, happiness, etc. They also
pray when Grandma gets sick, and when Grandma doesn't get
better (or dies), many end up disillusioned or bitter. This is because they don't understand what the Bible says about prayer. It
teaches, among other things, that our sin will keep God from
even hearing our prayer (Psalm 66:18), and that if we pray with
doubt, we will not get an answer (James 1:6,7). Most important,
God answers our prayer according to *His* will, not ours (1 John
5:14,15).

Here's how to be heard:

- Pray with faith (Hebrews 11:6).
- Pray with clean hands and a pure heart (Psalm 24:3,4).
- Pray genuine heartfelt prayers, rather than vain repetitions
  (Matthew 6:7).
- Make sure you are praying to the God revealed in the Scrip-
  tures (Exodus 20:3–6).

How do you "pray with faith"? Someone once told me, "Ray,
you're a man of great faith in God," thinking they were paying
me a compliment. They weren't. What if I said to you, "I'm a
man of great faith in my doctor"? It's a compliment to the doctor.
If I have great faith in him, it means that I see him as being a
man of integrity, a man of great ability—that he is trustworthy. I
give "glory" to the man through my faith in him. The Bible says
that Abraham "did not waver at the promise of God through unbelief, but was strong in faith, giving glory to God; and being
fully persuaded that, what he had promised, he was able also to
perform" (Romans 4:20,21). Abraham was a man of great faith in
God. Remember, that is not a compliment to Abraham. He mere-

ly caught a glimpse of God's incredible ability, His impeccable integrity, and His wonderful faithfulness to keep every promise He makes. Abraham's faith gave "glory" to a faithful God.

As far as God is concerned, if you belong to Jesus, you are a VIP. You can boldly come before the throne of grace (Hebrews 4:16). You have access to the King *because you are the son or daughter of the King*. When you were a child, did you have to grovel to get your needs met by your mom or dad? I hope not.

So, when you pray, don't say, "Oh God, I *hope* you will supply my needs." Instead say something like, "Father, thank You that You keep *every* promise You make. Your Word says that You will supply *all* my needs according to Your riches in glory by Christ Jesus [Philippians 4:19]. Therefore, I thank You that You will do this thing for my family. I ask this in the wonderful name of Jesus. Amen."

Hudson Taylor, a great missionary, said, "Prayer power has never been tried to its full capacity. If we want to see divine power wrought in the place of weakness, failure, and disappointment, let us answer God's standing challenge, 'Call unto me, and I will answer you, and show you great and mighty things of which you know not of.'"

How do you get "clean hands and a pure heart"? Simply by confessing your sins to God through Jesus Christ, whose blood cleanses from all sin (1 John 1:7–9). God will not only forgive your every sin, He promises to *forget* them (Hebrews 8:12). He will even justify you based on the sacrifice of the Savior. This means He will count it as though you have never sinned in the first place. He will make you pure in His sight—sinless. He will even "purge" your conscience, so that you will no longer have a sense of guilt that you sinned. That's what it means to be "justified by faith." That's why you need to soak yourself in Holy Scripture; read the letters to the churches and see the wonderful things God has done for us through the cross of Calvary. If you don't bother to read the "will," you won't have any idea what has been given to you.

How do you pray "genuine heartfelt prayers"? Simply by keeping yourself in the love of God. If the love of God is in you, you will never pray hypocritical or selfish prayers. Just talk to your heavenly Father as candidly and intimately as a young child, nestled on Daddy's lap, would talk to his earthly father. How would you feel if every day your child pulled out a pre-written statement to dryly recite to you, rather than pouring out the events and emotions of that day? God wants to hear from your heart. When your prayer-life is pleasing to God, He will reward you openly (Matthew 6:6).

How do you know you're praying to "the God revealed in Scripture"? Study the Word. Don't accept the image of God portrayed by the world, even though it appeals to the natural mind. A kind, gentle Santa Claus figure, dispensing good things with no sense of justice or truth, appeals to guilty sinners. Look to the thunderings and lightnings of Mount Sinai. Gaze at Jesus on the cross of Calvary—hanging in unspeakable agony because of the justice of a holy God. Such thoughts tend to banish idolatry.

5. Warfare—Praise the Lord and Pass the Ammunition

Before you became a Christian, you floated downstream with the other dead fish. But now that God has put His life within you, you will find yourself swimming against a current. When you became a Christian you stepped right into the heat of an age-old battle. You have a threefold enemy: the world, the devil, and the flesh. Let's look at these three resistant enemies.

Our first enemy is the world, which refers to the sinful, rebellious, world system. The world loves the darkness and hates the light (John 3:20), and is governed by the "god of this world" (2 Corinthians 4:4). The Bible says the Christian has escaped the corruption that is in the world through lust. "Lust" is unlawful desire, and is the life's blood of the world—whether it be the lust for sexual sin, for power, for money, for material things. Lust is a monster that will never be gratified, so don't feed it. It will grow bigger and bigger until it weighs heavy upon your back, and will be the death of you (James 1:15).

There is nothing wrong with sex, power, money, or material things, but when desire for these becomes predominant, it becomes idolatry. We are told, "Do not love the world, neither the things that are in the world. If any man loves the world, the love of the Father is not in him"; whoever is "a friend of the world makes himself an enemy of God" (1 John 2:15; James 4:4).

The second enemy is the devil, who is the "prince of the power of the air" (Ephesians 2:2). He was your spiritual father before you joined the family of God (John 8:44). Jesus called the devil a thief who came to steal, kill, and destroy (John 10:10).

The way to overcome him and his demons is to make sure you are outfitted with the spiritual armor of God (Ephesians 6:10–20). Become intimately familiar with it. Sleep in it. Never take it off. Bind the sword to your hand so you never lose its grip. The reason for this brings us to the third enemy.

The third enemy is what the Bible calls the "flesh." This is your sinful nature. The domain for the battle is your mind.

If you have a mind to, you *will* be attracted to the world and all its sin. The mind is the control panel for the eyes and the ears, the center of your appetites. All sin begins in the "heart" (Proverbs 4:23; Matthew 15:19). We think of sin before we commit it. James 1:15 warns that lust brings forth sin, and sin when it's conceived brings forth death. Every day of life, we have a choice. To sin or not to sin—that is the question. The answer is the fear of God. If you don't fear God, you will sin to your sinful heart's delight.

Did you know that God kills people? He killed a man for what he did sexually (Genesis 38:9,10), killed another man for being greedy (Luke 12:15–21), and killed a husband and wife for lying (Acts 5:1–10). Knowledge of God's goodness—His righteous judgments against evil—should put the fear of God in us and help us not to indulge in sin.

If we know that the eye of the Lord is in every place beholding the evil and the good, and that He will bring every work to judgment, we will live accordingly. Such weighty thoughts are valuable, for "by the fear of the Lord men depart from evil" (Proverbs 16:6).

Jesus said, "And I say to you, my friends, do not be afraid of those who kill the body, and after that have no more that they can do. But I will show you whom you should fear: Fear him, who after he has killed, has power to cast into hell; yes, I say to you, fear him!" (Luke 12:4,5).

6. Fellowship—Flutter by Butterfly

One evidence that you have been truly saved is that you will have a love for other Christians (1 John 3:14). You will want to fellowship with them. The old saying that birds of a feather flock together is true of Christians. You gather together for the breaking of bread (communion), for teaching from the Word, and for fellowship. You share the same inspirations, illuminations, inclinations, temptations, aspirations, motivations, and perspirations —you are working together for the same thing: the furtherance of the kingdom of God on earth. This is why you attend church —not because you have to, but because you want to.

Pray about where you should fellowship. Make sure your church home calls sin what it is: sin. Do they believe the promises of God? Are they loving? Does the pastor treat his wife with respect? Is he a man of the Word? Does he have a humble heart and a gentle spirit? Listen closely to his teaching. It should glorify God, magnify Jesus, and build up the believer.

Don't become a "spiritual butterfly." If you are flitting from church to church, how will your pastor know what type of food you are digesting? The Bible says that your shepherd is accountable to God for you (Hebrews 13:17), so make yourself known to your pastor. Pray for him regularly. Pray also for his wife, his family, and the elders. Being a pastor is no easy task. Most people don't realize how long it takes to prepare a fresh sermon each week. They don't appreciate the time spent in prayer and in study of the Word. If the pastor repeats a joke or a story, remember, he's human. So give him a great deal of grace, and double honor. Never murmur about him. If you don't like something he has said, pray about it, then leave the issue with God. If that doesn't satisfy you, leave the church, rather than divide it through murmuring and complaining. God hates those who cause division among the brethren (Proverbs 6:16–19).

A woman once spread some hot gossip about a local pastor. What he had supposedly done became common knowledge around town. Then she found that what she had heard wasn't true. She gallantly went to the pastor and asked for his forgiveness. The pastor forgave her, but then told her to take a pillow full of tiny feathers to a corner of the town, and in high winds, shake the feathers out. Then he told her to try to pick up every feather. He explained that the damage had already been done. She had destroyed his good reputation, and trying to repair the damage was like trying to pick up feathers in high winds.

The Bible says that there is life and death in the power of the tongue. We can kill or make something alive with our words. Pray with the psalmist, "Set a watch O Lord, before my mouth; keep the door of my lips."

7. Thanksgiving—Do the Right Thing

For the Christian, every day should be Thanksgiving Day. We should be thankful even in the midst of problems. The apostle Paul said, "I am exceedingly joyful in all our tribulation" (2 Corinthians 7:4). He knew that God was working all things together for his good, even his trials (Romans 8:28).

Problems *will* come your way. God will see to it personally that you grow as a Christian. He will allow storms, to send your roots deep into the soil of His Word. We also pray more in the midst of problems. It's been well said that you will see more from your knees than on your tiptoes.

A man once watched a butterfly struggling to get out of its cocoon. In an effort to help it, he took a razor blade and carefully slit the edge of the cocoon. The butterfly escaped from its problem . . . but immediately died. It is God's way to have the butterfly struggle. It is the struggle that causes its tiny heart to beat fast, and send the life's blood into its wings.

Trials have their purpose. They make us struggle in the cocoon in which we often find ourselves. They bring us to our knees. It is there that the life's blood of faith in God helps us spread our wings.

Faith and thanksgiving are close friends. If you have faith in God, you will be thankful because you know His loving hand is upon you, even though you are in a lion's den. That will give you a deep sense of joy, which is the barometer of the depth of faith you have in God. Let me give you an example. Imagine if I said I'd give one million dollars to everyone who ripped out the last page of this book and mailed it to me. Of course, you don't believe I would do that. But imagine if you did, and that you knew 1,000 people who had sent in the page, and every one received their million dollars—no strings attached. More than that, you actually called me, and I assured you personally that I would keep my word. If you believed me, *wouldn't* you have joy? If you didn't believe me—no joy. The amount of joy you have would be a barometer of how much you believed my promise.

We have so much for which to be thankful. God has given us "exceeding great and precious promises" that are more to be desired than gold. Do yourself a big favor: believe those promises, thank God continually for them, and "let your joy be full."

8. Water Baptism—Sprinkle or Immerse?

The Bible says, "Repent, and be baptized every one of you in the name of Jesus Christ for the remission of sins..." (Acts 2:38). There is no question about whether you *should* be baptized. The questions are how, when, and by whom?

It would seem clear from Scripture that those who were baptized were fully immersed in water. Here's one reason why: "John also was baptizing in Aenon near Salim, because there was much water there" (John 3:23). If John were merely sprinkling believers, he would have needed only a cupful of water. Baptism by immersion also pictures our death to sin, burial, and resurrection to new life in Christ. (See Romans 6:4; Colossians 2:12.)

The Philippian jailer and his family were baptized at midnight, the same hour they believed (Acts 16:30–33). The Ethiopian eunuch was baptized as soon as he believed (Acts 8:35–37), as was Paul (Acts 9:17,18). Baptism is a step of obedience, and God blesses our obedience. So what are you waiting for?

Who should baptize you? It is clear from Scripture that other believers had the privilege, but check with your pastor; he may want the honor himself.

9. Tithing—The Final Frontier

It has been said that the wallet is the "final frontier." It is the final area to be conquered—the last thing that comes to God in surrender. Jesus spoke much about money. He said that we cannot serve God and mammon (Matthew 6:24). "Mammon" was the common Aramaic word for riches, which is related to a Hebrew word signifying "that which is to be trusted." In other words, we cannot trust God and money. Either money is our source of joy, our great love, our sense of security, the supplier of our needs—or God is.

When you open your purse or wallet, give generously and regularly to your local church. A guide of how much you should give can be found in the "tithe" of the Old Testament: 10 percent of your income. Whatever amount you give, make sure you give *something* to the work of God (see Malachi 3:8–11). Give because you *want* to, not because you have to. God loves a cheerful giver (2 Corinthians 9:6,7), so learn to hold your money with a loose hand.

10. Troubleshooting—Cults, Atheists, Skeptics

If you know the Lord, nothing will shake your faith. It is true that the man with an experience is not at the mercy of a man with an argument. Take for example a little boy who is looking at a heater. His father warns him that it's hot. The child says, "Okay, I believe it's hot." At that point, he has an intellectual belief that the heater is hot. When his dad leaves the room, he says, "I wonder if it really is hot?" He then reaches out his little hand and grabs the heater bar with his fingers. The second his flesh burns he stops believing the heater is hot. He now *knows* it's hot! He has moved out of the realm of "belief" into the realm of "experience."

In comes a heater expert who says, "Son, I have a B.A. in the study of heat. The heater is definitely not hot. I can prove it to you." The child would probably say, "Mr. Expert, I don't care how many B.A.'s you have. I *know* that heater is hot—I touched it! I don't just believe it, I've experienced it. Goodbye."

If you have touched the heater bar of God's love and forgiveness, if the Holy Spirit has "born witness" that you are a child of God (Romans 8:16), if you have received the gospel with "power, the Holy Spirit and much assurance" (1 Thessalonians 1:5), you will *never* be shaken by a skeptic.

When cults tell you that you must do certain works to achieve salvation, don't panic. Merely go back to the Instruction Manual. The Bible has all the answers, and searching them out will make you grow.

If you feel intimidated by atheists—if you think they are "intellectuals"—read my book *How to Make an Atheist Backslide*. It will show you that they are the opposite. It will instruct you on how you can prove God's existence, and also prove that the "atheist" doesn't exist.

Finally, the way to prevent sports injury and pain is to keep yourself fit—exercise. The apostle Paul kept fit through exercise. He said, "Herein do I exercise myself, to always have a conscience void of offense toward God, and toward men" (Acts 24:16). Do the same. Listen to the voice of conscience. It's your friend, not your enemy. Remember these words of Solomon:

> "Fear God and keep His commandments: for this is the whole duty of man. For God shall bring every work into judgment, including every secret thing, whether it be good, or whether it be evil" (Ecclesiastes 12:13,14).

Keep the Day of Judgment before your eyes. On that Day, you will be glad for the cultivations of a tender conscience.

Thank you for taking the time to read this. I hope the principles expounded in it have been helpful, and that any knowledge you have gained from it will some day save you some pain.

Resources

. . . .

Products to help you grow in your faith

The Evidence Bible (Bridge-Logos Publishers). A comprehensive resource to help you share your faith and answer common objections to Christianity; offers hard evidence and scientific proof for the thinking mind. Commended by Josh McDowell, Dr. D. James Kennedy, and Franklin Graham.

Revival's Golden Key (Bridge-Logos Publishers). Learn how to share your faith biblically. "I have over one thousand books on evangelism, soul-winning, and revival in my personal library and none of them are worthy to be compared to this book." —R. W. Jones, Word of Truth Ministries

How to Make an Atheist Backslide (Bridge-Logos Publishers). Contrary to common thought, God's existence can be proven—simply and absolutely—without the use of faith or even the Bible. Designed to cause professing atheists to seriously doubt their doubts, this book will also encourage and strengthen the faith of believers.

Available through your local Christian bookstore

Hell's Best Kept Secret (audio). Listen to the "hottest message on the planet" freely at www.raycomfort.com.

For a complete list of books, tracts, tapes, and videos by Ray Comfort, visit our website at www.raycomfort.com, call 800-437-1893, or write to: Living Waters Publications, P. O. Box 1172, Bellflower, CA 90706.

 RAY COMFORT's ministry has been commended by Franklin Graham, Josh McDowell, Dr. D. James Kennedy, David Wilkerson, Bill Gothard, Joni Eareckson Tada, and many other Christian leaders. He has written for Billy Graham's *Decision* magazine and Bill Bright's *Worldwide Challenge*. He has preached in over 700 churches; his videos have been seen by more than 30,000 pastors; and millions of his gospel tracts are sold each year. Ray is originally from New Zealand, where he preached "open air" over 3,000 times before moving to the U.S. He has written more than 30 books, including *Hell's Best Kept Secret*, which has sold more than 100,000 copies. He and his wife, Sue, and their three grown children live in Southern California.